It's another Quality Book from CGP

This book is for anyone studying AQA GCSE Textiles.

Let's face it, D&T is pretty hard-going — you've got a whole load of technical stuff to learn on top of doing your project.

Happily this CGP book helps to take the headache out of all that learning. We've explained all the technical stuff — and drawn plenty of pictures to make the whole thing that bit clearer. Plus we've stuck in some handy hints to help make your project a winner, and some tips on exam technique.

And in true CGP style it's got some daft bits in to try and make the whole experience at least vaguely entertaining for you.

What CGP is all about

Our sole aim here at CGP is to produce the highest quality books — carefully written, immaculately presented and dangerously close to being funny.

Then we work our socks off to get them out to you — at the cheapest possible prices.

Contents

SECTION ONE — DESIGN

SECTION TWO — MATERIALS AND COMPONENTS

Project Advice

Unlike most subjects, in Textiles you actually get to <u>make something trendy</u> (well, hopefully).

The Project is Worth 60% of your GCSE

1) Your Textiles <u>project</u> is called 'the <u>controlled assessment</u>'.

2) There are <u>90 marks</u> available for the project (the folder plus the final product).

3) Your teacher will give you as much help as they're allowed to by the exam board, so do <u>ask them</u>... but mostly it's <u>up to you</u> to make a <u>good job</u> of your project.

4) You can dip into this book for a bit of extra help. Section 1 is all about the design process, so if you're not sure <u>where to start</u>, that might be a good place to look.

5) If you're wondering about a particular <u>detail</u> — the properties of <u>cotton</u>, say — it's probably quickest to look it up in the <u>index</u> and go straight to that page.

Only Put Relevant Stuff in Your Folder

1) Your teacher will give you plenty of guidance on what needs to go in your folder, but you can use this section of the book for a reminder.

Your project should take about 45 hours to complete, so plan your time carefully and don't take too long doing little things that won't earn you any marks.

2) The next two pages tell you <u>what you can get marks for</u> and give you a few tips on <u>how</u> to get them.

3) This next bit is <u>really important</u>:

- Don't waffle. Your folder should be about <u>20 sheets</u> of A3. You'll <u>lose marks</u> if you do much more than this.
- So <u>DON'T</u> waste space on <u>irrelevant</u> stuff, especially at the <u>research</u> stage (see next page).

Include Plenty of Photos

1) <u>DO</u> put in lots of <u>photos</u>. You <u>MUST</u> take photos of your final product, of course.

2) But also, take photos while you're <u>developing</u> your design (see next page)...

3) ...and during the <u>intermediate stages</u> of making your product, to show the making process.

Example

The fastenings need to be strong, so I'm using metal zips. It doesn't matter that they are bulky because denim is a heavy fabric.

The pockets are attached using double stitching to provide extra strength.

Controlled Assessment — nope, it's not funny...

When your project is marked, only about a <u>third</u> of the marks are for making the final thing and how good it is. Most of the controlled assessment marks depend on the <u>sheer brilliance</u> of your <u>folder</u>.

Project Advice

The Exam Board Sets the Task

You'll be given a <u>context</u> and a <u>design brief</u>.   For example:

> #### Context
> Tourist attractions like zoos and wild animal parks usually have their own gift shops.
> Animal-themed textile products are always popular gift items.
>
> #### Design Brief
> A local wild animal park has asked you to design a range of animal-themed children's products.
> You should present initial ideas for a range of products, including a rucksack and a pair of mittens.
> Develop and make one of your designs.

Task Analysis is Worth 8 Marks

You need to show that you've <u>understood</u> the task. To get <u>top marks</u> for this you'll have to:

* <u>Analyse</u> the <u>context</u> — e.g. show that you understand how the design of textile products can be influenced by different animals (e.g. fabrics, textures, colours and decorative techniques...).
* **Identify and research the <u>target market</u>** — e.g. find out what children are likely to want and need, and which animals appeal most to children (see pages 6-7 for more on market research).
* Analyse <u>existing products</u> — visit shops selling children's products and look online to research them. If possible, use product disassembly to figure out how existing products have been constructed... (see pages 4-5 for more on product analysis).
* <u>Analyse</u> your <u>research</u> — summarise your findings and say how they'll influence your design (see page 10 for more on research analysis).
* Write a <u>design specification</u> (see page 10) — make sure the criteria are <u>based on your research analysis</u>.

> But remember, this stuff is only worth 8 marks out of 90. The moderators <u>don't</u> want to see more than <u>three A3 sides</u> of research. However they <u>do</u> want you to <u>summarise</u> your findings and they <u>do</u> want you to <u>use your research findings</u> when you write your design criteria.

Development of Proposals is Worth 32 Marks

Your design folder should 'tell the story' of your design. The moderator wants to see how you got from the design specification to the manufacturing specification. So, make sure you:

* Come up with <u>creative</u> and <u>original</u> ideas — see pages 11-12.
* Use <u>CAD</u> where <u>appropriate</u>, e.g. to produce mood boards, design logos and stencils or draw and annotate your design ideas — see page 13.
* Show that you're taking <u>social</u>, <u>moral</u> and <u>environmental</u> issues into account — see Sections 1 and 3.
* <u>Model</u> your design and make improvements — see pages 14-17, and remember to take photos of the various things you've tried out.
* Explain <u>why</u> you've chosen particular <u>materials</u> and <u>components</u> — see Section 2.
* Write a fully detailed <u>manufacturing specification</u> and <u>production plan</u>, including quality control checks — see pages 18-19.

Tell the story of your design — and give it a happy ending...

You'd scarcely believe how much moderators <u>hate</u> wading through pages and pages of products that you've <u>printed off the internet</u>. Believe me, you won't get many 'research' marks if that's all you do.

Project Advice

Making is Worth 32 Marks

This is the really fun bit — actually making your product. So enjoy it, but remember:

1) Use all the quality control checks you put in your manufacturing specification.
   (If you don't, and you make a complete hash of things, you'll only have to start again.)

2) You'll only get top marks if you work accurately and skilfully. So use the right techniques and tools for the job, including CAM if appropriate, and don't be slapdash — it'll show.

3) Remember to take photos during the process, as well as of the finished thing.

4) Make sure you work safely and use tools correctly. Don't stick pins in people.
   Unless you're also doing GCSE Acupuncture.

Testing and Evaluating is Worth 12 Marks

To get those 12 marks you'll need to:

• Test and evaluate your design throughout the designing and making process, taking other people's opinions into account (see page 15).

• Refer back to the design and manufacturing specifications when you evaluate your ideas and product.

• Justify (explain why) you're making particular changes to the product.

• Explain how you'd modify the product for commercial production.

Communication is Worth 6 Marks

1) Moderators love it when you use the right technical words.

2) They love it even more if you spell things correctly and use good grammar and punctuation.

3) Make sure you've explained things clearly — get someone who knows nothing about your project to read it and see if it makes sense.

4) And remember, you won't get top marks for communication if you write too much or waffle.

Paula was disappointed to hear that her communication system was only worth 6 marks.

But Don't Forget The Exam — It's Worth 40%

1) In the exam you'll be tested on everything you've learned during the course — materials, tools, how to design things, how to make things, health and safety, environmental issues...

2) This book can help you learn all that stuff — and it has questions for you to check what you know.

3) There's a glossary at the back of the book, in case you need to sort out your microfibres from your micro-encapsulation.

4) The exam technique section (pages 60-63) has some worked examples of exam-style questions, and some hints on how to make sure you get top marks.

Evaaaaaaaal-u-ate good times, come on...

When you evaluate a design or product, remember to explain which aspects of the design or product need changing and why. It's another little step on the long and winding road to coursework heaven.

Product Analysis and Trends

The process of <u>designing</u> and <u>making</u> something is called '<u>the design process</u>' (oooooooh).
This process is <u>similar</u> in both <u>school</u> and <u>industry</u> — for one thing, it always starts with a <u>Design Brief</u>.

A Design Brief Introduces the Idea for a New Product

A designer is usually given a <u>design brief</u> by a <u>client</u> (e.g. a retailer).
This is a <u>statement</u> of the designer's <u>task</u>. It might include:

1) an <u>outline</u> of the <u>context</u> (background) and <u>who</u> the product is aimed at (the target group)

2) what <u>kind</u> of product is needed

3) how the product will be <u>used</u>

> Design Brief
> A specialist tie shop sells many different types of ties. Design and make a tie for a golf fan which could be sold in the shop.

The design brief is <u>short</u> and to-the-point — it's a <u>starting point</u> for the development of the product.

Analyse Other Products to Get Ideas for Your Own

Before you create a new textile product it's a good idea to <u>research past</u> and <u>present</u> products — this is called <u>product analysis</u>. This can expand your understanding of the type of product you'll be designing and gives you information on:

1) The <u>design</u> and <u>materials</u> used.

2) 'Tried and tested' <u>manufacturing techniques</u>.

3) Suitability for the <u>target market</u>.

You can use the <u>internet</u> to analyse products — online shops usually give lots of product information.

To <u>analyse</u> a textile product you need to look at <u>features</u> like the ones below.
Think about <u>both</u> the <u>good and bad</u> points and any <u>modifications</u> that could be made.

COMPONENTS
E.g. the tunic is <u>decorated</u> using <u>beads and sequins</u>. Other products might use <u>fastenings</u> such as <u>buttons</u>.

MATERIALS
E.g. the <u>finely-woven sheer fabric</u> used for these sleeves means they <u>hang well</u>.

SHAPE
E.g. the straight body shape is influenced by <u>trends</u> from the <u>1960s</u>.

DECORATIVE TECHNIQUES
E.g. adding <u>embroidery</u> or <u>printing</u> to the tunic would change how it <u>looks</u> and how it has to be <u>made</u>.

CONSTRUCTION TECHNIQUES
E.g. the <u>sleeve fabric</u> is <u>gathered</u> where it's <u>sewn</u> to the body.

FITNESS FOR PURPOSE
E.g. these sleeves are fine for <u>evening wear</u> but <u>wouldn't</u> be <u>practical</u> for <u>day wear</u>.

PRICE
E.g. this price would be OK for the target group of <u>wealthy professionals</u>.

All of these features contribute to the <u>marketability</u> of a product — how <u>well</u> the product will <u>sell</u>.

You can use this product information as a <u>basis</u> for designing your own product —
but think of ways to make <u>your product better</u> and more <u>appealing</u> to your target market.

This is your Design Brief — it will self-destruct in 15 seconds...

It's important to do research before you generate design ideas, so that you know what's already on the market. You can be inspired by other products — then think of ways to make yours unique.

Product Analysis and Trends

Disassembly Tells You How a Product was Made

1) Finding out how other products are <u>assembled</u> will help you to <u>choose</u> the <u>best methods</u> for making your own product. This means finding out:

- How parts of the product were <u>put together</u>.
- The <u>order</u> in which the parts were put together.
- How <u>decoration</u> was added to the product.

You could take apart the seam here to find out how the sleeve is attached.

You could look closely at the buttons to find out how they are securely attached.

2) You can do this by <u>disassembling</u> the product. This involves:

- <u>Examining</u> each <u>section</u> closely.
- <u>Taking the product apart</u> to see how it was put together.

You could look between the outer and lining of the jacket to see if it has an interlining. And if so, what material is used.

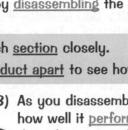

3) As you disassemble a product you'll be able to make <u>critical judgements</u> about how well it <u>performs</u> — whether it's <u>fit for purpose</u>. E.g. you could look closely at these buttons and make a judgement about how well they're secured to the coat.

4) Your critical judgements can give you ideas about how the product could be <u>improved</u>, which you can use in your own product design.

5) Disassembly can be an <u>expensive method</u> of product analysis, but it is often the <u>most effective</u> way of finding out about how a product has been constructed.

You can also <u>analyse</u> the <u>sales figures</u> of <u>similar products</u> to find out which ones are <u>selling well</u>, which <u>aren't</u>, the <u>seasonal differences</u> and what's the <u>most popular price</u>. You can use this information to plan <u>new designs</u>, and adaptions for a different season or market.

Trend Forecasts Predict Future Fashion Trends

As well as looking at products on the market <u>now</u>, you also need to know what will be <u>in fashion</u> when your product is <u>sold</u> in the <u>future</u>.

1) A <u>trend</u> is when fashions follow a <u>particular direction</u>, e.g. denim jackets, goth style, tulip skirts,...

2) Some people's jobs involve <u>predicting future fashions</u> — making <u>trend forecasts</u>.

3) <u>Trend forecasts</u> can be made quite far in <u>advance</u>, e.g. fabric forecasts might be made 18 months before products appear in the shops and colour forecasts 24 months ahead.

4) Designers <u>follow</u> trend forecasts so that they know <u>what other designers are likely to be doing</u> and to make sure their products are <u>up-to-date</u>. If a product's <u>on-trend</u>, it's more marketable — easier to <u>sell</u>.

5) Designers can keep up-to-date with forecasts by looking at <u>fashion forecast websites</u> and attending <u>fashion shows</u> and <u>trade shows</u>.

Practice Questions

1) <u>Who</u> writes a design brief and <u>what</u> is it for?

2) Sue wants to design a hat. She starts by analysing hats by another designer.
   a) Give <u>two</u> advantages for Sue of doing this.
   b) Suggest <u>three</u> features Sue could look at when analysing the hats.
   c) <u>Why</u> might it help her to <u>disassemble</u> the other designer's hats?

3) Javier is designing a shirt. He starts by analysing the different styles of shirt on the market.
   a) <u>Why</u> might Javier look at <u>sales figures</u> for the shirts?
   b) <u>How</u> can Javier make sure his design <u>won't</u> soon be <u>out-of-date</u>?

Market Research

As a designer you need to know what consumers <u>want to buy</u> (<u>consumer choice</u>), so that you can design a product that will <u>sell</u>. So, first of all you need to...

Identify Your Target Group

Even the very best products won't be everyone's cup of tea — some people will <u>like</u> them, some <u>won't</u>.

You might be given a <u>target market</u> in the design brief, or have a specific <u>target group</u> you want to design for. If not, you need to work out which people are <u>most likely</u> to buy your product — this should be your target group. Ask members of your target group <u>what they want</u> the product to be like.

You can group people by things like <u>age</u>, <u>gender</u>, <u>job</u>, <u>hobbies</u>, <u>lifestyle</u>, <u>money</u>, or anything else — it'll probably be a combination of a few of these things.

For example... if you're trying to sell <u>wide-legged, elasticated-waist, linen trousers</u>, you may decide to target them at <u>middle-aged women</u> who are buying their <u>summer clothes</u>.

EXAM TIP
In the exam, make sure you're <u>clear</u> on who your target group are before you start designing.

But, if you've designed some fetching <u>stripy knee-length socks</u>, you'd be better off targeting them at <u>teenage girls</u> in winter.

Think Carefully About What You Want to Find Out

Once you're clear on exactly who your target group are, you need to decide what to <u>ask</u> them. You could find out:

1) Some information about the <u>person</u> answering your questions. This could help you make sure they're within your <u>target group</u>, or give you <u>extra information</u>.
   - Are they male or female? (probably best to judge for yourself rather than asking...)
   - What age bracket are they in? (11-15, 16-20, 21-25 etc)
   - What job or hobbies do they have?

2) Do they already <u>buy</u> the kind of product you're thinking of developing?

3) Do they like a particular <u>style</u> or <u>colour</u>?

4) <u>How much</u> would they be prepared to pay for this kind of product? This could affect your <u>budget</u> — the lower the selling price, the lower the manufacturing costs will need to be to make a profit.

5) <u>Where</u> would they expect to buy it from? Again, this could affect costs. E.g. if the majority of your target group buy textile products from Primark® you should design a low-cost product.

6) Is there something they <u>would like</u> from the product that existing products <u>don't have</u>?

At a <u>later stage</u> in the design process, when you've generated <u>ideas</u>, you may decide to ask the target group <u>more questions</u>.

E.g. <u>will they buy your version of the product?</u> Explain the advantage of your product over existing brands — would that be enough to tempt them to buy your version?

They never stock clothes in my size...

My target group is tall, dark and handsome...

Like it or not you need to know your target group really well — you'll feel like friends by the end of the design process. This is a really important stage — you need to be confident people will buy your stuff.

Market Research

Now, how to phrase those all-important <u>questions</u>...

Questionnaires are Forms for People to Fill In

There are two basic types of question:

1) <u>CLOSED QUESTIONS</u> — these have a <u>limited</u> number of possible answers,
e.g. '<u>do you ever use a bag?</u>' can only be answered 'YES' or 'NO'.
Analysing is easy and you can show clear results at the end. Closed
questions include <u>multiple choice questions</u> — these give a <u>choice</u> of
answers. Sometimes the person answering can pick more than one. E.g.

> Q4.   Which of these types of bag do you own?
> Satchel ☐   Clutch ☑   Rucksack ☑

2) <u>OPEN QUESTIONS</u> — these have <u>no set answer</u>, e.g. <u>what's your favourite type of bag, and why?</u>
They give people a chance to provide details and opinions. This type of questioning takes more time
and it's harder to draw conclusions from the results. But you could gain valuable information.

Interviews are Face-to-Face Conversations

1) For interviews, you can <u>start off</u> by asking the same sort of questions as in questionnaires
— but then take the chance to ask <u>follow-up</u> questions, based on the answers you get.

2) Get your interviewees to give you <u>extra information</u> to explain their answer — this might help you
get more <u>ideas</u> for your product. E.g. if their favourite hat is a beret, ask them <u>why</u> they like it.

3) Interviews can give you more <u>detailed</u> information than questionnaires
— you can have short <u>conversations</u> with people you're aiming to sell to.
Just make sure you <u>stick to the point</u>.

4) A problem with interviews is that it's often more <u>difficult</u> to <u>analyse</u> the results than with questionnaires
— it's harder to <u>compare opinions</u> when the topics covered vary slightly from person to person.

ICT can Help you Research and Present Information

1) You could write a <u>questionnaire</u> using <u>word processing</u> software — so it'll be <u>neat</u> and easy to read.
You could post it on a <u>website</u> that your <u>target group</u> is likely to use, so they could fill it in <u>online</u>.

2) You could use <u>spreadsheets</u> to <u>organise and sort data</u> (e.g. your questionnaire results).
Spreadsheets also allow you to <u>present</u> the data using <u>charts</u> and <u>graphs</u>.

3) You could use the <u>internet</u> to look up <u>sales figures</u> (see p. 5) and collect them in a <u>spreadsheet</u>.

Practice Questions

1) You are designing a <u>babygrow</u>, so you go to a parent and baby group to talk to the <u>parents</u>.
   a) In market research, what is the name for this set of people?
   b) Think of <u>three useful questions</u> you could <u>ask them</u> about the babygrows <u>they buy</u>.

2) a) Jordan plans to <u>interview</u> people for her market research. She needs to know <u>whether</u> people
   buy flip-flops and the most popular <u>sizes</u> and <u>colours</u>. Peter says using a <u>questionnaire</u> to get
   the answers to these questions might be better. <u>Is Peter right?</u> Explain <u>why</u>.
   b) Jordan decides to broaden her questions to ask about <u>what sort</u> of beach shoes people <u>most</u>
   <u>like</u>, and <u>why</u>. Describe the <u>potential benefits</u> and <u>drawbacks</u> of using this <u>type of question</u>.

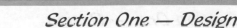

Section One — Design

Consumer Choice and Product Design

Product design is influenced by many things. One of the biggest influences is what people want to buy — consumer choice. And that's affected by all sorts of factors...

Product Design is Affected by...

① ...Developments in Technology...

1) Manufacturing has advanced so that products can be made more quickly and cheaply. This has encouraged consumers to buy clothes that they only wear a few times before throwing away.

2) Many people carry MP3 players or mobile phones, so they're keen to buy products that can hold these devices, e.g. many bags have internal mobile phone pockets.

3) Fabrics that are developed for use in specialist fields, like the military or by astronauts, eventually become available for use in consumer clothing. E.g. GORE-TEX® is a breathable but waterproof fabric that was used in spacesuits in the 1980's, but is now found in a lot of outdoor clothing.

② ...Fashion Trends...

Fashion trends can now change every few weeks, instead of twice a year for the traditional Autumn/Winter and Spring/Summer fashion collections. They can be short-lived or be fashionable for a long time, e.g. the 'little black dress'. Consumers who follow the latest fashion will buy according to the current trend, so designers have to keep up with this.

③ ...Economic Factors...

Deidre didn't need another hat, but this one would be perfect for the office.

RICH ECONOMY

People have more disposable income, which they can spend on luxury and impulse buys, e.g. a leather jacket, tailored shirts or a new handbag they don't really need.

POOR ECONOMY

People have less disposable income (e.g. in wartime or a recession) and are more likely to spend their money on essentials, e.g. knickers, socks, work clothes. Some people will buy cheaper products to reduce costs, whereas others will invest in just a few expensive, better-quality products that will last longer.

④ ...Social Factors...

1) Newspapers and magazines are often full of features about what celebrities are wearing — this can lead to new trends.

2) People are living longer and older people may have different requirements from textile products, e.g. they may prefer shoes with lower heels and wider fittings for comfort.

3) Peer pressure can affect consumer choice, e.g. kids all wearing the 'hoodie' in order to fit in.

4) Lifestyle or work also affects what people buy, e.g. a lawyer might need lots of smart suits.

What I really, really want... is a pink fluffy waistcoat...

If it wasn't for fashion, I could still be wearing my shell suit. Hmmpf. Lots of factors there for you to understand and absorb. And what's this I see on the horizon? More factors — I think it is you know...

Consumer Choice and Product Design

5 ...Cultural Factors...

Product design can be affected by <u>cultural</u> factors — like <u>tradition</u>, <u>religion</u> and <u>the arts</u>. For example:

1) <u>Traditional</u> Indian female dress includes <u>saris</u>, which come in different colours and patterns.
2) Some <u>religions</u> don't believe women should show bare skin outside the home — so bikinis wouldn't have a market in these cultures.
3) Some consumers will buy products that reflect the latest <u>music/pop culture</u>, e.g. band t-shirts.
4) <u>Different cultures</u> also affect <u>international fashion trends</u>, e.g. in summer 2009 one of the trends included tribal patterns on female clothes and accessories.
5) Textiles design can be influenced by the work of other <u>artists</u> — e.g. Pop Art in the 1950s.

6 ...Ethical Trading...

Some consumers are <u>concerned</u> about the <u>welfare</u> of people who <u>make</u> the textile products in our shops. They want to buy <u>ethically traded</u> products. This means that the people who make the products are <u>not exploited</u> (taken advantage of) — that they work in <u>safe</u> conditions and are paid <u>fairly</u>. People are often willing to <u>pay more</u> to buy ethically traded products. These products are often <u>labelled with symbols</u> so that consumers can identify them.

Designers have a <u>responsibility</u> to consider how the production of their product will affect the <u>people</u> involved. E.g. they should think about:
- The <u>materials</u> used — and whether they are ethically produced.
- <u>Where the product is made</u> — it's <u>cheaper</u> to have products made <u>abroad</u> but some countries employ <u>children</u> in <u>sweat shops</u> where the conditions are very poor.

7 ...Environmental Sustainability...

See p. 44-45 for more ethical and environmental issues.

Some consumers are worried about the effect of textiles production on the <u>environment</u>. They want to buy <u>sustainable</u> products. <u>Sustainability</u> means <u>not</u> using up <u>finite</u> resources or causing <u>permanent damage</u> to the environment. Sustainable textiles design might include using fabric made from <u>renewable</u> sources (sources that <u>won't run out</u>) such as bio fibres (see p. 45), using <u>cleaner</u> technology in manufacturing and <u>minimising waste</u>.

'Finite' means it will run out.

Designers have a <u>responsibility</u> to think about the <u>environmental</u> impacts of their products. E.g. the <u>product's life cycle</u> (how it's made, used and disposed of) — aspects of the product's life cycle may <u>harm the environment</u> and be <u>unsustainable</u>.

8 ...and Ethical Design Issues

Designers also have a responsibility to consider the product's <u>ethical/moral design</u>. E.g. <u>children's clothing</u> shouldn't be too <u>sexy</u> or have <u>rude slogans</u> on it — textile products need to be <u>appropriate</u> for the <u>age</u> of their <u>target group</u>.

Practice Questions

1) People are more likely to buy <u>cheap clothes</u> that are <u>not expected</u> to <u>last a long time</u> today, than they used to be. Give <u>three</u> reasons for this.
2) Explain why products produced by a <u>less ethical</u> manufacturer might <u>cost less</u> than those made by a manufacturer who practises <u>ethical trading</u>.
3) Describe <u>two</u> steps designers and manufacturers can take to ensure that their textiles products are <u>made as sustainably as possible</u>.

Generating Design Ideas

Here it is folks, the answer to your burning question of what to do with all that <u>research</u>...

Draw Conclusions From Your Research

Once you've done some <u>product analysis</u> and <u>market research</u> (pages 4-7), you should have loads of information. Now it's time to use it — this is called <u>research analysis</u>:

1) <u>Describe</u> how you did your research and what you hoped to find out, e.g. "I asked 45 people aged 8-11 to fill in my questionnaire to find out what style of socks they liked most".

2) <u>Summarise</u> what you've found out — pick out the most important and useful findings, e.g. "animal designs are popular for socks".

3) <u>Explain</u> what impact the research will have on your designs, e.g. "animals will be a major theme".

4) <u>Suggest</u> ways forward from the research you've done, e.g. "one idea would be to make the socks represent animals themselves by adding eyes and a nose".

Then Write a Design Specification

1) The <u>conclusions</u> from your market research and product analysis should show what kind of <u>characteristics</u> your product needs to have.

2) Write up these characteristics as a detailed list of <u>design criteria</u>. This list is called a <u>design specification</u>.

3) Include points to cover some or all of the following:

• aesthetics (shape, size, colour etc.)	• safety/ethical issues	• fabrics (i.e. properties & features)
• how it will be used	• theme	• components
• financial constraints	• target market	• construction & decorative techniques

The <u>fabric specification</u> — see p. 31.

4) Each point says <u>one thing</u> about what the product should be like.
E.g.

> Design Specification for a Reusable Shopping Bag
> * The finished bag must be retailed for £3 or less.
> * It must be made out of environmentally friendly material.
> * It must be brightly coloured.
> * It must appeal to young people.
> * It must be strong enough to hold shopping.
> * It must be lightweight.
> * It must fold down to fit into another bag.
> * It must have a secure pocket.
> Etc...

"You could make a bag just like mine. (Just don't tell anyone the handle broke)."

5) The criteria must be <u>related to your research</u> — e.g. you could say "the bag should feature hearts", but <u>only</u> if your research analysis concludes that <u>people want</u> a bag with hearts on it — <u>don't</u> just make it up because it sounds interesting.

6) The design specification is a <u>starting point</u> from which you can <u>generate</u> your <u>design ideas</u>.

7) Throughout the design process you'll need to <u>refer back</u> to the <u>design specification</u> and <u>evaluate</u> your product designs against it (see p. 14). The <u>final product design</u> must meet <u>all</u> the points on the specification.

Design specs aren't a type of fancy glasses...

So research isn't something you do just for the sake of it — it's important you draw <u>useful conclusions</u>. These will help you to decide what your product should be like and to write the <u>design specification</u>.

Generating Design Ideas

Right, time to get your <u>creative</u> juices flowing and think of some <u>design ideas</u>...

There are a Few Tricks that Can Help You Get Started

1) You could create a <u>mood board</u> — this is a load of different images, words, materials, colours and so on that might trigger ideas for a design.

2) Work from an <u>existing product</u> — but change some of its features or production methods so that it fits in with your <u>design criteria</u>.

3) Or you could do a spot of <u>brainstorming</u> (see below).

The outcome of a successful brainstorm for casual weekend-wear...

Brainstorm to Produce Initial Ideas

1) First, think up <u>key words</u>, <u>questions</u> and <u>initial thoughts</u> relating to your product. Use the <u>design specification</u> criteria to guide you.

2) <u>Don't</u> be too <u>critical</u> at this stage — let your <u>imagination</u> run wild. Even if an idea sounds ridiculous, put it down anyway. Be <u>creative</u> and get <u>as many ideas</u> as you can.

3) Afterwards, decide which ones are <u>good</u> (and so are worth developing) and which ones are as <u>stupid</u> as a holey umbrella.

You can do quick sketches as you brainstorm.

Design Criteria:
- RRP £3 or under
- environmentally friendly material
- brightly coloured
- appealing to young people
- strong enough for shopping
- lightweight
- can fold down
- secure pocket

Key words:

foldable   young   bright
cheap
environment   lightweight
pocket   strong

Red, heart-shaped bag with side zip

Thick plastic bag with clear pockets for photos

Large blue hemp bag with flower pattern — folds in half

IDEAS FOR A REUSABLE SHOPPING BAG

Stripy A4 cotton bag with cord handles

Purple net bag — fully foldable

Pet kangaroo — use its pouch when shopping

Questions:
How can it be light AND strong?

Can plastic be environmentally friendly?

What kind of patterns are popular with young people?

Practice Questions

1) 250 people have completed your <u>questionnaire</u> about the size of their head and their favourite hat colour. What should you do with this information <u>before</u> you write a <u>design specification</u>?

2) You are briefed to design a CGP tea towel. Suggest <u>five design criteria</u>.

3) You are asked to design two new products. For <u>each one</u>, suggest <u>why</u> the given method is a <u>sensible</u> way to come up with initial ideas.
   a) A <u>lighter and more fashionable</u> rucksack for day trips — work from <u>existing products</u>.
   b) Quilt covers and pillowcases <u>inspired by</u> Art Deco and 1920s fashions — use a <u>mood board</u>.

Generating Design Ideas

Now that you've <u>sorted</u> out your <u>good ideas</u> (like the stripy cotton bag) from your bad ones
(a kangaroo would definitely cost too much to keep), you need to <u>sketch</u> the good ones out <u>clearly</u>.

You Need to Come Up with a Range of Designs

1) You need to present <u>a few different</u> designs that <u>meet</u> the <u>design criteria</u>.
   In the <u>exam</u> you'll do <u>two</u>. You'll need to do <u>more</u> for your <u>project</u>.

2) You might want to <u>combine</u> the <u>best features</u> from a few of your <u>initial</u> ideas to generate a <u>really good</u>
   <u>idea</u>. E.g. looking at the brainstorm on the previous page, the heart bag may be popular with young
   people, but the stripy cotton bag may be more practical — so you could have a cotton bag with a
   heart motif... lovely.

3) When <u>presenting</u> your ideas, it's usually
   best to keep it simple — a <u>freehand</u>
   <u>pencil sketch</u> will do fine, as long
   as it's <u>clear</u> and <u>neat</u>.

4) If you're <u>confident</u>, you could try
   something a bit posher, like a 3D drawing.

5) It's important that you think you could
   actually <u>make</u> your design ideas
   — don't go overboard on exciting ideas
   that you could never produce for real.

Design Ideas for a Reusable Shopping Bag
First Idea

Organic cotton fabric
— this is lightweight,
environmentally friendly
and foldable

Brightly coloured,
stripy pattern
— will appeal to
young people

Thick black cord
— for strong handles

Metal eyelet
— to prevent
the fabric fraying
or tearing

Front pocket
— for small
shopping
purchases, mobile
phone, or purse

Embroidered heart motif
— will appeal to young people

6) <u>Annotate</u> (i.e. add <u>notes</u> to) each
   design idea to fully <u>explain</u> what it is
   and why it's <u>good</u>. You could mention:

• fabrics	• components	• decorative techniques
• user	• colours	• construction techniques
• shape	• fitness for purpose	• special features

Make sure you relate these features back to the <u>design criteria</u>.

Choose Your Best Design Idea to Develop

Have a good <u>think</u> about all your design ideas and decide which is the <u>best</u> — i.e. the one that most
<u>closely matches</u> the design brief and design specification. This is the idea you should <u>develop</u>.

Now you need to present a <u>more detailed</u> version of your <u>final design idea</u>.

Include:

<u>Sketches</u> — a <u>front and back view</u> of your design

<u>Annotation</u> — <u>label</u> anything that's <u>not clear</u> on your
sketches and write <u>more detailed notes</u> explaining how
your design <u>fits</u> the <u>design specification</u>.

EXAM TIP
In the exam you'll be told <u>what</u>
<u>features</u> of your final design you'll
be given marks for, so <u>read them</u>
<u>carefully</u> and cover them all.

Wearing white in the rain — not a good idea...

The design you choose to develop needs to <u>fit</u> the <u>design specification</u> — so you end up with a product
that your <u>client wants</u> and that your <u>target group</u> will <u>buy</u>. Otherwise, Houston, we have a problem...

Generating Design Ideas

Computers pop up everywhere nowadays — and they come in very handy with product design.

Use CAD to Help You Design and Develop Ideas

1) Computer-Aided Design (CAD) involves designing products on a computer, rather than using the traditional method of sketching on paper.

2) CAD software includes 2D painting software (e.g. Adobe® Photoshop® and Corel PHOTO-PAINT®), 2D drawing software (e.g. Adobe® Illustrator® and CorelDRAW®) and 3D modelling software (e.g. Pro/DESKTOP®).

3) You can use CAD to:

Produce mood boards (see p. 11) to help generate ideas.

Draw and annotate your initial and final design ideas.

Design logos, stencils, fabric prints and transfers. E.g. you could design a fabric print using a paint programme or by collecting an image on a digital camera. The design can then be manipulated on screen (e.g. the colours changed) and then used to produce 'virtual reality samples'.

Model your final design in 3D — a 'virtual prototype', which will let you see if the design is working.

Communicate with your client — you could present your final idea to your client using a 'virtual catwalk' to make sure it's what they want. You could also email CAD images to them throughout the design process to keep them informed.

Draw the pattern pieces for your design and work out how best to lay them out on the material (the 'pattern lay plan') to minimise waste.

Calculate how to change a pattern to make different sizes of a garment (this is called 'pattern grading').

JAMES KING-HOLMES / SCIENCE PHOTO LIBRARY

Practice Questions

1) Rodney is doing a practice exam. These are his design ideas for an environmentally friendly, cool, summer shirt. What four major things are wrong with his design idea drawings?

2) Give two ways you could use CAD to help you produce design ideas.

3) Explain how computers can be used to include the client in the design process.

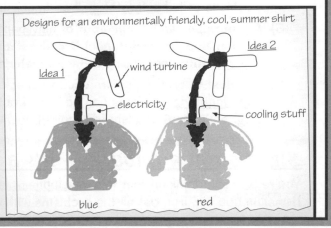

Designs for an environmentally friendly, cool, summer shirt

Idea 1   Idea 2

wind turbine

electricity

cooling stuff

blue   red

Development

So you've decided which idea to develop and drawn it out nicely, but I'm afraid that's not the end of the matter. Now you need to test out your design — and then make <u>improvements</u> to it.

You Should Test and Evaluate Your Design...

1) You need to <u>test</u> your product design to make sure it <u>does what you want it to do</u> — that it fits the <u>design specification</u>. This is the <u>evaluation</u>. It's best to go through the design criteria one by one.

2) You'll probably find that parts of your design <u>don't work out</u> the way you wanted them to or don't fit the <u>design specification</u>. If so, you need to <u>think</u> about the <u>improvements</u> you could make to the design.

> <u>Design Specification for a Reusable Shopping Bag</u>
> - The finished bag must be retailed for £3 or less.
> - It must be made out of environmentally friendly material.
> - It must be brightly coloured.

E.g. maybe the reusable shopping bag <u>looks great</u> but the organic, stripy cotton is actually too <u>expensive</u>. You could find a <u>cheaper alternative</u> stripy, organic fabric, or you could use white organic cotton and <u>dye it yourself</u> — using a natural dye. Both of these ways mean the product still fits the specification.

1 ...By Making More Detailed Sketches...

You could use CAD to help you here.

1) More <u>detailed</u> drawings of your design might show the construction techniques (e.g. seams), the <u>texture</u> of the fabric or the <u>exact design</u> of a <u>print</u>, <u>logo</u>, or <u>decoration</u> (e.g. beading).

2) Detailed sketches let you <u>test</u> how your product will <u>look</u> before making a model (see below).

3) You can <u>try several versions</u> of particular <u>details</u> and get <u>feedback</u> on them.
E.g. you could draw sketches of several different heart motifs and ask young people which they like best — the favourite one would then be used in your final product.

2 ...By Modelling...

Modelling is about <u>trying out</u> your design, so you can work out the <u>details</u> and <u>identify</u> problems.

1) You can try out different <u>decorative designs</u> or <u>construction techniques</u> on small <u>samples</u> of fabric.

2) You can model <u>different aspects</u> of your design (e.g. a sleeve, a pocket) to <u>experiment</u> with different shapes, fabrics and components.

E.g. model the pocket on the reusable shopping bag to test how different fastenings work with the fabric.

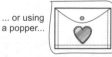 using a zip... 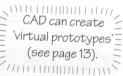 ... or using a popper...

3) As you're modelling, you need to make the <u>paper pattern pieces</u> for your product — the <u>templates</u> you'll use for cutting out the fabric pieces.

CAD can create 'virtual prototypes' (see page 13).

4) It's a good idea to make a <u>full-scale model</u> of your product design — this is called a "<u>prototype</u>" or "<u>mock-up</u>" (in fashion it's called a "<u>toile</u>").

5) A prototype can be made out of <u>newspaper</u>, <u>recycled fabric</u> or <u>calico</u> (cheap, white cotton often used in industry prototypes) because it's just used to test the <u>size</u> and <u>shape</u>. You could make <u>several</u> prototypes, using different materials, to find the best drape or overall look.

6) In industry, prototypes are used to check on the <u>manufacturing methods</u> so any potential <u>manufacturing problems</u> can be sorted out. They're also used to help <u>plan mass production</u> (e.g. equipment and labour required, manufacturing time and costs, etc.).

Sir, it's not a doodle — it's a detailed sketch for D&T...

You're probably thinking that this development lark is a slow process, but it's a really important one. It means you can iron out all the problems with your design before you make it for real.

Development

3 ...By Considering Other People's Views...

User trials

These involve asking a <u>sample</u> of your <u>target market</u> to <u>try out</u> your prototype. Their <u>feedback</u> will help you <u>modify</u> your design so that it's <u>appealing</u> to the target market, is <u>fit for purpose</u> and will <u>sell</u> (hopefully). E.g. young people might test the resuable shopping bag prototype and say that the cord handles make the empty bag bulky to carry around.

Use <u>questionnaires</u> or <u>interviews</u> to get feedback (see p. 7).

Cotton fabric straps instead of cord.

Reinforced stitching for strength.

Expert opinions

Experts are other <u>professionals in the textiles industry</u> (e.g. designers, seamstresses, haberdashers, fabric store owners). You can <u>benefit</u> from their <u>experience</u> by asking them to look at your design and <u>suggest improvements</u>. E.g. if you're making an evening dress a seamstress might be able to suggest ways to alter your pattern to make it cheaper and easier to make, but still look as good.

The client

Early on in the development of your design idea it's helpful to show a <u>prototype</u> to your <u>client</u> to make sure it fits the <u>image</u> they had in mind for the product.
If it's not what they had in mind, the design can be changed <u>before</u> manufacturing starts.

4 ...And by Comparing Your Design to Similar Products

You could disassemble products to help you analyse them (see p. 5).

1) Look at a selection of <u>similar</u> products that are already <u>on the market</u>.

2) Think about how the <u>fabrics</u>, <u>components</u>, <u>shapes</u>, <u>sizes</u> and <u>styles</u> make these products <u>attractive</u> to your <u>target market</u> and <u>fit for purpose</u>.

3) Use these evaluations to make <u>improvements</u> to your own product design.

This shopping bag is fit for purpose — it's a large size and made of strong hemp.

This bag has a pocket which is useful for storing small items but the colour is unappealing.

This beach bag is fit for purpose — the fabric is waterproof.

The bright decoration on this bag would appeal to young people.

Practice Questions

1) When you're <u>evaluating</u> your final design, <u>what</u> should you <u>check its features against</u>?

2) Karen is designing oven gloves for her project. She draws <u>several</u> designs with <u>different styles</u>, but isn't sure which would be most <u>popular</u>. How could she <u>find out</u>?

3) What is a <u>prototype</u>?

4) Give <u>three</u> things that <u>prototypes</u> are used for in <u>industrial textiles production</u>.

5) You've made a <u>prototype</u> of a bag for <u>carrying snowboards</u>.
   a) Describe <u>why</u> it would be worthwhile getting some snowboarders to try it out.
   b) <u>Who else</u> might it help to show it to before you start final production, and why?

Development

I can see you're having too much fun being creative with this. So it's time to mention a couple of less exciting (but important) stages of development — thinking about <u>costs</u> and <u>methods</u> of <u>manufacture</u>.

You Need to Work out the Cost of Production

1) During the development process you need to keep track of <u>costs</u>, so you don't end up with a final design that costs <u>far too much</u> to make. The design specification should include a criteria on cost.

2) Making <u>models</u> and <u>prototypes</u> will help you calculate some of the <u>manufacturing costs</u> — e.g. the costs of materials. In industry, there are also lots of <u>indirect</u> costs to consider too.

> **COSTS**
> - <u>materials</u> and <u>components</u>
> - <u>labour</u> (including <u>training</u> etc.)
> - <u>packaging</u>
> - <u>energy</u> and <u>waste disposal</u>
> - cost of <u>new equipment</u>
> - cost of <u>transporting</u> products

You can use spreadsheets to help you work out costings.

You may have to work within certain <u>constraints</u>:

- <u>BUDGET</u> — e.g. if your client has a <u>small</u> budget you might have to <u>modify</u> some of your design features to <u>cut costs</u>. For example, you could simplify the design so that it uses less fabric.
- <u>TIMESCALE</u> — you need to <u>balance</u> this with costs. E.g. if the product needs to be made <u>quickly</u>, <u>higher labour costs</u> might need to be paid for overtime. Or, more money could be budgeted for <u>equipment</u>, say, if it'll save time and costs in the long term by making sure the product's ready on time.

You Can Adapt Your Design to Manufacture in Quantity

You might have to <u>modify</u> your design, so it can be made easily in bulk — be careful it doesn't lose its <u>originality</u> though. For example, by <u>changing</u> the:

Mass (or batch) production is where a <u>huge number</u> of your product will be made (see p. 56), often using <u>assembly lines</u> and <u>computer-controlled machines</u>.

<u>STYLE</u> — so it's <u>simpler</u>. E.g. a pleated skirt could be made with <u>fewer pleats</u> so it's <u>quicker</u> to make.

<u>FABRICS AND COMPONENTS</u> — so they're more easily <u>available</u> to manufacturers and <u>affordable</u> for the mass market. E.g. a <u>silk</u> dress could be made out of a <u>synthetic</u> material, which is cheaper.

<u>DECORATIVE EFFECTS</u> — so they're <u>less labour intensive</u>. E.g. a <u>beaded pattern</u> on an evening bag could be simplified and made <u>repetitive</u>, so it's <u>quick and easy</u> to stitch on.

<u>METHODS OF ASSEMBLY</u> — could be reordered. E.g. different parts of a design could be <u>made separately</u>, like the <u>sleeves</u> of a shirt, then attached towards the end of the production process. This is called <u>sub-assembly</u>.

Designer dresses are adapted for mass production and sold on the high street, for much lower prices.

That's a 'no' to the chocolate-dispensing attachment, then...

Sadly you can't always be as creative as you'd like to be with this designing lark — you might be restricted by <u>financial</u>, <u>time</u> or <u>manufacturing</u> constraints. Just one more page on development to go...

Development

You need to keep <u>testing</u> and <u>modifying</u> until you create the <u>'perfect' product</u>,
or at least as perfect as you can make it...

Keep Going Until You Get it Just Right

You might find that you end up modifying something, then trying it out, then making <u>another</u> modification and trying that out, then making <u>another</u> modification and trying that out, and so on.

That's just the way it goes sometimes. Depending on your time and resources, you could make any number of <u>alternative</u> models/prototypes. Then go back and select the <u>best</u> one.

Here's a summary of how it works <u>every time</u> you try something new:

| Make a model | → | Test and evaluate | → | Come up with ideas to change the product | → | <u>Remember to check</u> your final prototype against the design specification. |

QUALITY ASSURANCE

The process of <u>testing</u> your product, <u>evaluating</u> it against the specification and <u>modifying</u> your design to make it better is called <u>quality assurance</u>. It means you end up with a <u>quality product</u> — one that is safe, fit for purpose, correctly priced and that fits the design criteria from your client. It's in yours and your client's interest to create a quality product so that people will <u>buy</u> it and buy from your brand/company in the <u>future</u>. Quality assurance <u>continues</u> in the <u>manufacturing</u> process (see p. 58).

Keep a Record of Your Evaluations

1) When you're doing this for real with your own product, you need to keep a <u>record</u> of <u>what you find out</u> from each model and the <u>changes</u> you make to your design as a result.

2) It's a great idea to use a <u>digital camera</u> to record all the <u>models</u> and <u>samples</u> you make — you could even create a <u>database</u> of the photos and modifications on a computer.

3) As your design changes write down <u>how</u> and <u>why</u> it <u>fits</u> the <u>design specification</u>. E.g. replacing the cord handles with cotton straps means the bag will fold down more easily.

EXAM TIP
In the exam, you might be asked to evaluate how well your design meets a criteria from the specification — make sure you give a detailed answer.

Practice Questions

1) Explain <u>why</u> it's <u>important</u> to think about <u>manufacturing costs</u> as part of the design process.

2) Give <u>three</u> examples of <u>costs</u> to consider when manufacturing a textiles product.

3) <u>Explain</u> how working to a certain <u>timescale</u> could lead to <u>increased</u> manufacturing <u>costs</u>.

4) Paulo has designed a <u>pleated</u> skirt with a <u>beaded and embroidered</u> pattern around the waistline. Suggest <u>how</u> Paulo could <u>adapt</u> his design so that it could be produced in <u>bulk</u>.

5) a) Explain how <u>quality assurance</u> forms part of the <u>design</u> process.
   b) How does quality assurance <u>benefit</u> both the <u>designer</u> and the <u>client</u>?

6) Hester has produced a <u>final prototype</u> for her novelty car seat cover (aimed at successful, young footballers). What should she <u>check</u> it against to make sure the product will be <u>fit for purpose</u>?

Planning Production

Now you're happy with your design, you need to tell the manufacturer how to make it.

You Need to Make a Manufacturing Specification...

A manufacturing specification can be a series of written statements, or working drawings and sequence diagrams. It should include a product specification, as well as manufacturing instructions. It needs to cover every detail, so that everyone involved in making the product knows exactly what they're doing and will produce high quality, consistent products. You need to compare your final prototype/sample to the manufacturing specification to make sure it's exactly right.

Product Specification:

1) **Fabric** and **component** details (including types, precise amounts, colours, finishes, etc.)
2) Details of any decorations to be applied.
3) A working drawing — a detailed drawing of the finished product with its precise dimensions in millimetres (see below).
4) Tolerances — margin of error for each measurement
5) Seam allowances — gap between edge of fabric and sewing line

You could also include detailed drawings of construction techniques, or attach fabric samples.

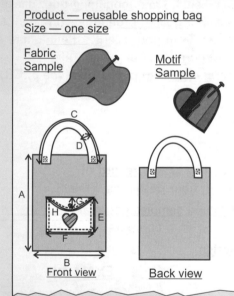

Product — reusable shopping bag
Size — one size

Fabric Sample

Motif Sample

Front view

Back view

Garment details

A. Height of bag	400 mm ± 5	E. Pocket height	150 mm ± 2
B. Width of bag	350 mm ± 5	F. Pocket width	200 mm ± 2
C. Length of strap	500 mm ± 2	G. Flap width	50 mm ± 1
D. Width of strap	20 mm ± 1	H. Flap length	250 mm ± 1

Seam allowance	10 mm ± 2

Materials:

Fabric for main part of bag	Plain blue organic cotton
Straps and pocket	Plain white organic cotton
Thread	Black cotton
Fastenings	1 popper (8 mm diameter)
Embroidered motif	Pre-made by 'Motifs-R-Us' (60 x 45 mm)

Manufacturing Instructions:

1) **How** to make it — a clear description of each stage of production
2) **Equipment** — what's needed for each stage
3) **Pattern lay plans** — often produced using CAD
4) **Costings** — a breakdown of all the costs
5) **Labelling** — the type of care/safety labels and how they'll be attached
6) **Packaging** — the type of packaging needed
7) **Quality control** instructions — where, when and how products should be checked during the manufacturing process for quality and safety

D'oh — no-one told me I'd have to do maths...

Here we are at the end of the design process... but don't rush this bit. The manufacturing specification needs to be detailed enough for someone to make your product without ~~messing it up~~ messing it up.

Planning Production

Manufacturing a product takes a shed load of careful <u>planning</u>.

...And be Able to Plan the Whole Process

When planning the production process you can use a <u>flow chart</u> to work out a <u>logical</u> and <u>efficient</u> sequence of tasks. You need to work out <u>how long</u> each task will take, and how these times <u>fit into</u> the <u>total</u> production time. This flow chart shows the kind of things to include:

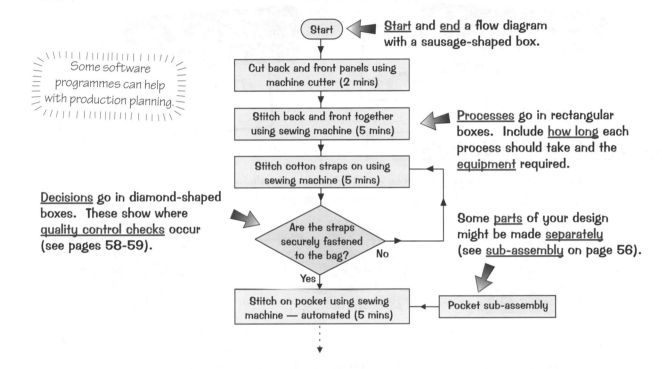

Some software programmes can help with production planning.

<u>Start</u> and <u>end</u> a flow diagram with a sausage-shaped box.

<u>Processes</u> go in rectangular boxes. Include <u>how long</u> each process should take and the <u>equipment</u> required.

<u>Decisions</u> go in diamond-shaped boxes. These show where <u>quality control checks</u> occur (see pages 58-59).

Some <u>parts</u> of your design might be made <u>separately</u> (see <u>sub-assembly</u> on page 56).

Quality Assurance is Important in Manufacturing Too

1) During the manufacturing process you need to make sure that the product <u>fits</u> the <u>manufacturing/product specification</u> — so <u>quality control checks</u> are built into the process. There's lots more on this in Section Four (pages 58-59).

2) When you've made <u>your final product</u>, you need to go through the process of <u>testing and evaluating</u>, all over again. Does it meet the <u>original design specification</u> and do what it's <u>supposed</u> to?

3) As part of the process, it's a good idea to get <u>other people's opinions</u> of the final product too.

Practice Questions

1) A manufacturing specification contains a detailed <u>product</u> specification. What <u>else</u> does it need to include?

2) Suggest what <u>details</u> about the <u>fabric</u> you should include in a product specification.

3) Describe what is meant by <u>tolerance</u>.

4) The following questions are about using <u>flow charts</u> in production planning.
   a) What does a <u>diamond-shaped</u> box show?
   b) The first process box on Tania's flow chart says to 'cut out the fabric pieces'. What <u>additional information</u> should she include with this <u>process</u>?

Section One — Design

Types of Fibre

Now to the stars of the show — the <u>fabrics</u>. First up, the <u>fibres</u> and <u>yarns</u> that fabrics are made from.

Yarns Are Threads Made From Tiny "Hairs" Called Fibres

1) <u>Fibres</u> come in either <u>short</u> lengths (<u>staple fibres</u>), or <u>longer</u> lengths (<u>filaments</u>). Filaments can be <u>cut up</u> into staple lengths if required.

2) <u>Staple</u> fibres are <u>spun</u> (twisted together) to produce <u>yarns</u>. Filaments can be <u>spun</u> or used <u>as they are</u>.

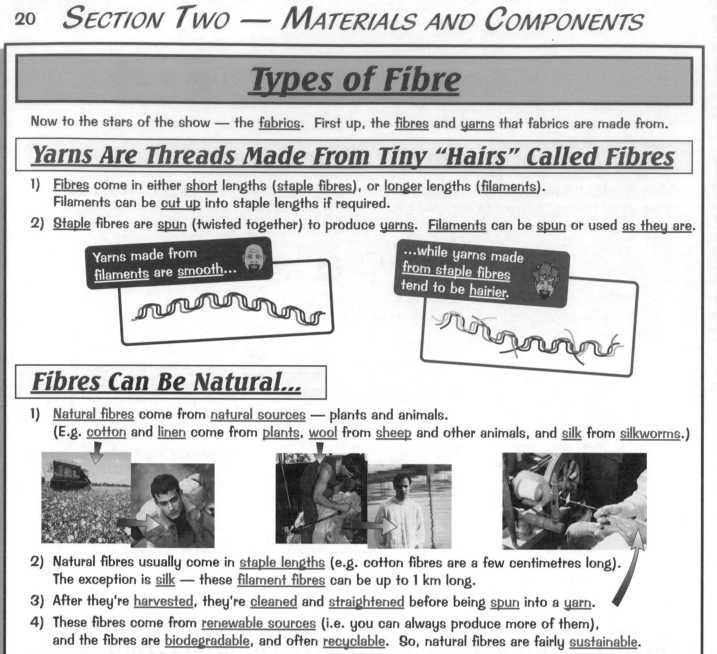

Yarns made from <u>filaments</u> are <u>smooth</u>...

...while yarns made <u>from staple fibres</u> tend to be <u>hairier</u>.

Fibres Can Be Natural...

1) <u>Natural fibres</u> come from <u>natural sources</u> — plants and animals. (E.g. <u>cotton</u> and <u>linen</u> come from <u>plants</u>, <u>wool</u> from <u>sheep</u> and other animals, and <u>silk</u> from <u>silkworms</u>.)

2) Natural fibres usually come in <u>staple lengths</u> (e.g. cotton fibres are a few centimetres long). The exception is <u>silk</u> — these <u>filament fibres</u> can be up to 1 km long.

3) After they're <u>harvested</u>, they're <u>cleaned</u> and <u>straightened</u> before being <u>spun</u> into a <u>yarn</u>.

4) These fibres come from <u>renewable sources</u> (i.e. you can always produce more of them), and the fibres are <u>biodegradable</u>, and often <u>recyclable</u>. So, natural fibres are fairly <u>sustainable</u>.

5) In general, natural fibres are <u>absorbent</u> and <u>strong</u> when dry, but have <u>poor resistance</u> to <u>biological damage</u>, e.g. from moths and mould.

...Regenerated...

1) <u>Regenerated fibres</u> are made from <u>natural materials</u> (usually <u>cellulose</u> from <u>wood pulp</u>) that are <u>chemically treated</u> to produce <u>fibres</u>.

2) <u>Different fibres</u> are made by using different <u>chemicals</u>.

3) For example, <u>viscose fibres</u> are made by <u>dissolving cellulose</u> in <u>sodium hydroxide solution</u>. This liquid is forced through tiny <u>holes</u>, and <u>hardened</u> to form <u>filament fibres</u>. These filaments are <u>stretched</u> into a <u>yarn</u> which is <u>wound</u> onto spools, or <u>chopped</u> into <u>staple lengths</u>.

4) The fibres have a <u>renewable origin</u>, but many are made using <u>synthetic chemicals</u>, which makes them <u>less sustainable</u> than natural fibres. However, some regenerated fibres, like <u>Tencel</u>®, are produced so that almost all of the <u>chemicals</u> used can be <u>recycled</u>, and the fibres are <u>recyclable</u> and <u>biodegradable</u>.

5) Regenerated fibres tend to have <u>similar properties</u> to <u>natural</u> fibres, but can be given different <u>properties</u> by using different <u>chemicals</u>. E.g. viscose is made to drape well.

Rapunzel, Rapunzel — let down a yarn of many staple lengths...

Your clothes may not seem quite as glam once you know that they're made from chemically treated wood pulp... But you still need to <u>learn</u> about <u>where</u> different fibres come from and <u>how</u> they're made.

Types of Fibre

...Or Synthetic

1) <u>Synthetic fibres</u> are man-made fibres.

2) They're made from <u>polymers</u> — <u>long chains</u> of <u>molecules</u>. These molecules come mainly from <u>coal</u> or <u>oil</u>. E.g. <u>polyester</u>, <u>LYCRA</u>® and <u>acrylic</u> are produced from <u>oil</u>, and <u>nylon</u> is produced from <u>coal</u>.

3) The polymers are <u>melted</u> or <u>dissolved</u> in solution. This <u>liquid</u> is then forced through tiny <u>holes</u> and <u>hardened</u> to form <u>filament fibres</u>.

4) The <u>filaments</u> are <u>stretched</u> into a <u>yarn</u> which is <u>wound</u> onto spools, or <u>chopped</u> into <u>staple lengths</u>.

5) Because they're made from <u>non-renewable sources</u>, they're <u>less sustainable</u> than other types of fibre.

6) Synthetic fibres can be given many <u>different properties</u>. In general, they're <u>resistant</u> to <u>biological damage</u>, and can be <u>changed by heating</u> to form different shapes (e.g. permanent pleats) and textures. However, they're <u>not very absorbent</u>, so they can be hard to <u>dye</u>.

There's lots more on the <u>properties of fibres and fabrics</u> on pages 24-25.

No matter what they threw at him, the new, synthetic James Bond just wouldn't dye.

Practice Questions

1) Fibres come as staple lengths or filaments. Which of the two is <u>longer</u>?

2) The picture to the right shows a close up of a section of yarn. Would you expect this yarn to have been made from <u>filaments</u> or <u>staple fibres</u>? <u>Explain</u> your answer.

3) Explain what makes <u>natural fibres</u> more <u>sustainable</u> than other types of fibre.

4) <u>Describe</u> how a <u>yarn of wool</u> is produced.

5) What are many <u>regenerated fibres</u> made from?

6) Give <u>two advantages</u> of <u>synthetic fibres</u>.

7) Geoffrey is designing a pair of shorts. He wants to <u>dye</u> the fabric a bright colour. Explain <u>why</u> Geoffrey <u>shouldn't</u> use a fabric made from <u>synthetic</u> fibres.

8) Which is the <u>tastiest</u> source of fibre — bran flakes or prunes?

Fabric Construction

Fabrics are made from yarns (held together by weaving or knitting), or fibres which are stuck together.

Fabrics can be Made from Woven Yarns...

Different woven fabrics are made by interlacing two sets of yarns — the weft, which travels from right to left (purple in the diagrams below), and the warp, which travels up and down the weave (green in the diagrams below).

PLAIN WEAVE

1) The simplest weave — the weft yarn passes over and under alternate warp yarns, making it unpatterned.

2) It's hard-wearing — strong and holds its shape well. It has a smooth finish (making it good for printing on).

3) It's the cheapest weave to produce and is used to make loads of fabrics, especially cotton-based ones.

over

under

The edge of a woven piece of fabric, where the weft yarns wrap around the warp yarns, is called the selvedge.

TWILL WEAVE

1) A twill weave creates a diagonal pattern on the surface of the fabric. E.g. the weft yarn goes over two yarns and under one. The next weft yarn repeats this, but one warp yarn further along.

2) It's stronger and drapes better than plain weave. It's used for fabrics such as denim.

over

under

SATIN WEAVE

1) The weft yarn goes over four or more warp threads and under one.

2) The long weft yarns on the surface (called floats) catch the light, so satin weave makes shiny fabrics (like satin).

3) But the floats can snag, so the fabric is quite delicate and doesn't resist abrasion.

over   under

float

...Non-woven Fibres...

Non-woven fabrics are layers of fibres held together by bonding or felting. They don't fray, and can be cut in any direction — which means there's little waste when laying out patterns. However, they don't stretch and aren't very strong.

BONDED FABRICS

1) These are "webs" of fibres held together by glue, stitches, needle-punching or heat.

2) They're used for interfacing (see p. 43), artificial leathers and disposable cloths (e.g. medical masks).

Stitch-bonded non-woven fabric

fibres

stitching

FELTED FABRICS

1) Felting is an older way of making non-woven fabric. Felt is made by combining pressure, moisture and heat to interlock a mat of wool fibres.

2) Felt can be used for carpet underlay, craft material, hats, jewellery and snooker table coverings.

Aren't fabwics twilling — we'd be beweft without them...

It's easy to know warp from weft, 'cos weft goes from weft to right (tee hee). The rest needs some careful learning, but with practice you'll soon be able to spot a twill weave at 50 metres...

Fabric Construction

...or Knitted Yarns

Knitted fabrics are made by interlocking one or more yarns together using loops.
These loops trap air, making knitted fabrics good insulators. They also stretch more than woven fabrics.
There are a couple of types you need to know about:

Weft-knitted fabrics

1) The yarn runs across the fabric, making interlocking loops
   with the row of yarn beneath.
2) These fabrics stretch and can lose their shape easily.
3) If the yarn breaks it can unravel and make a 'ladder'.
4) Weft-knit fabrics can be produced by hand or machine.
5) They're used for jumpers, socks and T-shirts.

Warp-knitted fabrics

1) The yarns run "up" the fabric, in loops, which interlock vertically.
2) They're stretchy but still keep their shape.
3) These fabrics are hard to unravel and are less likely to ladder.
4) They're made by machine — and the machines can be expensive.
5) Tights, swimwear, fleeces, and some bed sheets
   are all made from warp-knitted fabrics.

Disassemble Fabrics to Find Out How They're Made

1) You can pick a fabric apart to see how it's constructed.
   Examine it closely as it comes to pieces*.

2) If the yarns run straight, it's woven.
   To work out which type of weave it is, count how many warp
   yarns the weft yarns cross before they go underneath one.

3) If the yarns loop around each other in a repeated pattern, it's knitted.
   Weft-knitted fabrics will have a simpler pattern than warp-knitted ones.

4) If there are no yarns, just fibres, it's non-woven. Try to see what's holding the fibres together.

Hmm... under, over, under, over.
It's undoubtedly plain weave, Watson.

Practice Questions

1) In a woven fabric, in which direction does:
   a) the weft yarn travel?
   b) the warp yarn travel?

2) Describe what is meant by the selvedge on a woven fabric.

3) State the type of weave which:
   a) is the cheapest to produce.
   b) creates a diagonal pattern on the surface of the fabric.
   c) has long weft yarns on the surface called floats.

4) Martial arts expert Egbert wants to design some trousers that stretch
   but don't lose their shape. Should Egbert use weft-knitted or
   warp-knitted fabric?

*Not recommended for your mum's best linen, sister's dress, etc...

Fibres and Fabrics

Now to the properties of fabrics made from natural and regenerated fibres.

	FIBRE	USED IN THESE FABRICS	CHARACTERISTICS IN FABRICS			USES
			APPEARANCE	GOOD POINTS	BAD POINTS	
NATURAL FIBRES	COTTON (from seed pods of cotton plant)	E.g. denim, corduroy, calico	Smooth	Strong (even when wet), hard-wearing, absorbent, comfortable to wear, feels quite cool in hot weather, easy to wash & add colour to, doesn't cause allergies, non-static, fairly cheap.	Creases easily, high flammability, poor elasticity, can shrink when washed, dries slowly.	Jeans, T-shirts, blouses, soft furnishings.
	WOOL (from sheep's fleece)	E.g. knitted fabrics, Harris Tweed, gabardine, jersey, felt	Soft or coarse.	Warm, absorbent, good elasticity, low flammability, crease resistant, available in lots of fabric weights.	Can shrink when washed, dries slowly, can feel itchy, fairly expensive.	Suits, jumpers, coats, dresses, carpets.
	LINEN (from stalks of flax plant)	Linen	Natural look	Strong (even when wet), hard-wearing, absorbent, comfortable to wear, feels very cool in hot weather.	Creases badly, high flammability, poor elasticity, doesn't hang nicely (poor drape), can be expensive.	Trousers, summer suits, dresses, furnishings.
	SILK (from silkworm cocoons)	E.g. organza, chiffon, satin	Very smooth and glossy.	Smooth, absorbent, good drape, low flammability, comfortable to wear.	Creases easily, might not wash well, weak when wet, expensive.	Lingerie, underwear, dresses, shirts, ties.
REGENERATED FIBRES	VISCOSE (from wood pulp treated with sodium hydroxide & other chemicals)	E.g. rayon	Smooth, light, and glossy.	Absorbent, soft, comfortable to wear, easily washable, good drape, fairly cheap.	High flammability, not very hard-wearing, poor elasticity.	Lingerie, underwear, dresses, suits, linings, soft furnishings.
	ACETATE (from wood pulp treated with acetic acid & other chemicals)		Smooth and glossy.	Soft, comfortable to wear, easily washable, good drape, resists biological/sun damage, fairly cheap.	High flammability, not very hard-wearing, poor elasticity, not very absorbent	Linings, soft furnishings.

> When some fabrics rub together, a small electric charge (static) can build up.

Why does it always rayon me — this Harris Tweed dries slowly...

You'll need to justify your fabric selections in your designs, so learn these properties. Next synthetics...

Fibres and Fabrics

Next, properties of fabrics made from <u>synthetic</u> fibres...

FIBRE	USED IN THESE FABRICS	CHARACTERISTICS IN FABRICS			USES
		APPEARANCE	GOOD POINTS	BAD POINTS	
<u>POLYESTER</u> (produced from oil)	E.g. dacron	Smooth, can have lots of different finishes.	Strong (even when wet), hard-wearing, low flammability, good elasticity, cheap, resists creasing, dries quickly, resists biological damage.	Not absorbent, not biodegradable, damaged by strong acids, melts as it burns (so very harmful if clothes catch fire).	Sportswear, bed sheets, curtains, cushions, padding, table cloths.
<u>ELASTANE</u> (produced from oil)	E.g. LYCRA®	Soft	Extremely elastic (stretches up to 7 times its length), strong, hard-wearing, lightweight, keeps its shape well, resists sun/biological damage.	Not absorbent, high flammability, not biodegradable.	Sports/swim wear, underwear, combined with other fibres to add stretch.
<u>POLYAMIDE</u> (produced from coal)	E.g. nylon	Can be made with lots of different finishes.	Strong, hard-wearing, warm, good elasticity, crease resistant, good biological resistance, fairly cheap.	Not very absorbent, damaged by sunlight, melts as it burns.	Sportswear, furnishings, carpets, tights, socks.
<u>ACRYLIC</u> (produced from oil)		Similar to wool.	Strong (except when wet), soft, warm, insulating, good elasticity, crease resistant, lightweight, doesn't shrink, cheap.	Not very absorbent, high flammability, affected by static, pilling (balls of fibres on the surface) can occur.	Fake fur, knitted clothes, furnishings.

> Elastane is an example of an <u>elastomeric</u> fibre — a highly elastic fibre.

Practice Questions

1) State the <u>fibre</u> used to make these <u>fabrics</u>:
   a) denim   b) gabardine   c) chiffon

2) Give <u>two positive</u> and <u>two negative</u> properties of a fabric made from:
   a) 100% cotton   b) 100% wool

3) a) Give an example of an <u>elastomeric</u> fibre.
   b) State <u>one positive</u> and <u>one negative</u> property of the fibre you named in part a).

4) Suggest why <u>polyester</u> is often used to make <u>night clothes</u>.

5) Henry wants a fabric that feels <u>cool</u> in warm weather to use for a pair of <u>summer trousers</u>.
   a) Suggest a suitable fabric that Henry could use.
   b) Identify one <u>drawback</u> in using this fabric.

6) Steve has just completed his design for a pair of <u>boxer shorts</u> made from Harris Tweed. Give a reason why this is <u>not</u> an appropriate fabric to use for boxer shorts and suggest a <u>more suitable</u> alternative.

Combining Fibres in Fabrics

You might think you know the <u>properties</u> of every type of <u>fibre</u> by now, but you're not finished yet. But don't worry, these aren't <u>new types</u> of fibre — you're just learning about <u>mixing fibres together</u>.

Useful Fabrics Can Be Made by Combining Fibres

A fabric made from <u>one type of fibre</u> (e.g. 100% cotton) might not have <u>all the properties</u> you want for your product. Fabrics made from a <u>combination of different fibres</u> can give you <u>better</u> characteristics. But, <u>watch out</u> — you can also get some <u>less desirable</u> characteristics mixed in.

There are <u>several reasons</u> why you might want to combine fibres, such as:

1 APPEARANCE
You can create interesting <u>colour effects</u>, e.g. by using fibres with different levels of <u>absorbency</u> — the fibres will take up different amounts of dye, creating different tones. You can also create interesting <u>textures</u>, e.g. by using some smooth fibres and some which are rougher.

2 PRACTICAL QUALITIES
You might need to make your fabric <u>more hard-wearing</u> — you could do this by including <u>more durable fibres</u>.
Or you could make a fabric <u>more crease resistant</u>, e.g. by adding <u>synthetic fibres</u>.

3 WORKING QUALITIES
You could get your fabric to <u>drape</u> better, or to keep its <u>shape</u>, by including fibres that have those properties.

4 COSTS
You might want to combine fibres to <u>reduce costs</u>. For example, combining an <u>expensive</u> fibre (e.g. silk) with a <u>cheaper one</u> (e.g. cotton), often means you can keep many of the <u>characteristics</u> of the <u>expensive</u> fibre but in a <u>cheaper</u> fabric — making your product easier to sell.

Fibres Can Be Combined by Blending or Mixing

There are two ways of <u>combining</u> fibres to get fabrics with combined properties — <u>blending</u> fibres within yarns, and <u>mixing</u> different yarns (where each yarn is made from one type of fibre). Here's how:

BLENDING
1) A <u>blend</u> is when two or more <u>different fibres</u> are combined to produce a <u>yarn</u>.
2) These fibres are blended before or during <u>spinning</u>.
3) This mixed yarn is then <u>woven</u> or <u>knitted</u> to make a fabric.

MIXING
1) A <u>mix</u> is when a fabric is made up of two or more <u>different types of yarn</u>.
2) For example, you could weave a fabric using one type of yarn for the <u>warp</u> and another for the <u>weft</u>.

Mixed fibres — not like putting prunes on your bran flakes...

...I prefer to blend up a smoothie for breakfast anyway. Make sure you <u>learn</u> the advantages of combining fibres and the <u>two different ways</u> that you can do it — by <u>mixing</u> and <u>blending</u>...

Combining Fibres in Fabrics

Here are Some Examples...

EXAMPLE — BLENDED FIBRES

A combination of <u>cotton</u> and <u>polyester</u> fibres is one of the most common <u>blended</u> fabrics.

Cotton	Polyester
Hard-wearing & fairly strong	Hard-wearing & very strong
Absorbent	Not absorbent
Soft	Not very soft
Dries slowly	Dries quickly
Creases easily	Doesn't crease
Shrinks easily	Doesn't shrink
Highly flammable	Not very flammable

Polyester-cotton can be used for loads of things — from bedclothes to shirts and jackets.

By <u>blending</u> polyester and cotton fibres you can create a fabric that:
- is even <u>stronger</u> and remains <u>hard-wearing</u>
- is <u>less absorbent</u> — so dries more quickly
- is <u>soft</u> and <u>comfortable</u>
- resists <u>creasing</u> (is easier to iron)
- <u>doesn't shrink</u> easily
- but is <u>very highly flammable</u>

Watch out for <u>negative</u> properties.

The blend is an <u>easy care</u> fabric — it's easy to wash, dry and needs little or no ironing.

Other examples include blending wool with <u>nylon</u> to make more <u>hard-wearing</u> carpets, and blending <u>silk</u> with <u>polyester</u> to make fabric that has the <u>qualities</u> of <u>silk</u>, but is <u>cheaper</u> and <u>easier</u> to care for.

EXAMPLE — MIXED FIBRES

<u>Elastane</u> (LYCRA®) is commonly <u>mixed</u> with <u>cotton</u> — to make a <u>stretchier</u> fabric.

Cotton	Elastane (LYCRA®)
Absorbent and soft	Not absorbent
Not stretchy	Stretchy
Strong	Crease resistant

Cotton-elastane mixtures are often used for swimwear and tight-fit jeans.

EXAM TIP:
Make sure you give <u>specific</u> examples of how the properties change when you combine fibres. Don't just say it's "cheaper".

By <u>mixing</u> elastane and cotton yarns you can create a fabric that:
- remains <u>strong</u>
- <u>stretches</u> to fit snugly
- is <u>comfortable</u> to <u>move</u> in
- <u>resists creasing</u>
- can be <u>dyed</u> easily

You can also mix different yarns to create <u>decorative</u> effects — e.g. different <u>colours</u> of silk can be mixed to create two-tone <u>taffeta</u>, or <u>metallic</u> yarns can be mixed in to create <u>glittery</u> fabrics.
<u>Ripstop</u> fabrics are made by weaving thick <u>nylon</u> fibres into <u>cotton</u>, <u>silk</u> or <u>polyester</u> to add <u>strength</u>.

Practice Questions

1) Give <u>four reasons</u> why you would <u>combine fibres</u> to make a fabric.

2) What <u>type</u> of <u>fibres</u> would you use to make a fabric more <u>crease resistant</u>?

3) Describe the <u>two ways</u> of <u>combining fibres</u> in fabrics.

4) Give <u>three advantages</u> of using a blend of cotton and polyester to make a fabric, rather than just cotton.

5) How are <u>ripstop</u> fabrics made?

New Fabrics and Technologies

Now for some really, really, really, really, small fibres — and the clever things being done with fibres and fabrics.

New Fibres and Fabrics are Constantly being Developed

1) KEVLAR® is a very strong polymer that's made chemically and can be spun into strong fibres. The fibres are woven to give a fabric that's really, really strong and resistant to abrasion. It's used in bulletproof vests and clothing for motorcyclists.

2) NOMEX® is another polymer that's spun into fibres. It's very fire-resistant and is used in firefighters' clothing and racing drivers' overalls.

3) TENCEL® is a modern, regenerated, fibre. It combines the best properties of natural and synthetic fibres, and can be given many different textures. Its properties make it ideal for a variety of textiles — from luxurious bed sheets to non-woven wipes with a high wet strength. It's also made in an environmentally friendly way — by using sustainable wood pulp and minimising energy use and waste.

4) The FASTSKIN® swimsuit has been developed by Speedo®. It's designed to mimic a shark's skin — the rough surface reduces drag in the water to allow the swimmer to go faster.

5) More 'green' fibres are being developed from natural sources — e.g. bamboo and hemp.

Microfibres are Tiny and Really Useful

1) Microfibres are really thin fibres — they can be up to 100 times thinner than human hair.

2) They're usually synthetic fibres such as polyester or polyamide.

3) They're very versatile — they can be woven, knitted, or bonded to make fabrics.

4) Microfibres can be woven so tightly that they stop water droplets from penetrating, but let water vapour (e.g. sweat) escape — so the fabric is water repellent and breathable.

5) Microfibres are expensive, so they're often blended with cotton, linen or silk to reduce costs.

6) Microfibre-based fabrics are soft, comfortable to wear, last well and hang beautifully. They're used to make underwear, sportswear, hosiery (e.g. tights) and outdoor clothing.

Micro-encapsulation Lets You Put Chemicals in Fabrics

1) Micro-encapsulation is where a tiny droplet of chemical is coated in a shell — called a microcapsule.

2) These microcapsules can be embedded in microfibre fabrics, to give the fabric different properties.

3) Chemicals like perfumes, insect repellents, vitamins and odour neutralisers can all be embedded in fabrics using this method.

4) Examples of products that use this technology are antibacterial socks and scented lingerie.

Laminated Fabrics are made up of Layers

Lamination is another method of improving a fabric's properties. Laminated fabrics are made up of two or more different layers that are stuck together. Lamination can be used with more delicate fabrics — to add strength from an under layer, or protection from an outer layer. It can also add useful properties to a fabric, e.g. a layer of foam could be used to make a fabric more insulating.

> **EXAMPLE**
>
> A GORE-TEX® membrane contains lots of tiny pores which allow water vapour (i.e. perspiration) to escape, but are too small for bigger rain droplets to pass through — it's both waterproof and breathable. A GORE-TEX® product is made by laminating a GORE-TEX® membrane between an outer and an inner layer of fabric. This makes the product sturdier. This material is used in loads of outdoor clothing.

Lamb-ination — so that's how sheep keep the rain out...

There are loads of clever things you can do with textiles. I've made a special camping suit — it keeps rain and midges out, stops you sweating, feeds you breakfast and keeps you smelling good at all times.

New Fabrics and Technologies

Fabrics are being made which Conduct Electricity

Conductive fabrics are starting to be used to integrate electronics into textile products.
They conduct electricity through conductive fibres or coatings, while still being comfortable to wear.
Conductive fabrics can supply power to a range of components. Applications include:

- Sensors in clothes that monitor heart rate and blood pressure.
- Washable electronic switches integrated into clothing to operate things like MP3 players and mobile phones.
- Fabric that acts as an electrical heater — used in things like car seats and motorbike clothing.

Conductive fabrics are 'smart' if they react automatically to different conditions — see below.

Smart Fabrics Change Their Properties

Smart fabrics are designed to react automatically to changes in the surroundings. They can be produced using the techniques on these pages. E.g. these fabrics are made using micro-encapsulation:

Thermochromic fabric

1) Micro-encapsulated dye changes colour at different temperatures.
2) The colour changing effect is lost after 5-10 washes because the microcapsules burst.

Photochromic fabric

1) This changes from one colour to another in response to different light conditions.
2) It's used in fashion T-shirts and camouflage military clothing.

Nanomaterials may be Popular in the Future

Nanomaterials include fabrics made from nanofibres, or from regular fibres that have been modified using nanotechnology.

Nanofibres Nanofibres are often made from carbon or synthetic polymers. They're very, very, very thin and light, but are also very strong. They're often made into non-woven, felt-like sheets. Potential applications include lightweight, bulletproof vests.

Nanotechnology

1) Existing fibres and fabrics can be modified using nanotechnology to give them new properties.

2) Thin layers of nanoparticles (extremely tiny particles of a substance) can be attached to common fibres and fabrics. The layers are so thin that unlike conventional finishes, they don't change the feel of the fabric.

3) This technology is already being used to create antibacterial fabrics by attaching nanoparticles of silver. These fabrics have lots of medical uses, e.g. face masks and dressings, and can even be used for odour-free socks.

4) Another development is fabric that is coated with nanoparticles that will resist and break down dirt and stains — making self-cleaning fabrics.

Nanotechnology involves tinkering with substances on a really small scale. Nanoparticles of a substance often behave differently to regular particles.

Practice Questions

1) What type of new fabric would be most useful for:
   a) overalls for a refuelling mechanic?
   b) kneepad covers for a skateboarder?

2) Suggest three applications for a conductive fabric.

3) Explain what is meant by a smart fabric.

4) Describe how a fabric can be given insect-repelling properties.

Choosing Fabrics

Woah... I bet your head's swimming with all the different <u>fibres</u> and <u>fabrics</u> that there are. Well don't fret, because now you're going to find out how to pick the best fabric for a product...

Choose a Fabric That's Fit For Purpose...

1) A <u>textile product</u> must do the <u>job</u> it's designed to do — it must be <u>fit for purpose</u>.

2) When <u>choosing</u> a <u>fabric</u>, you need to decide which of the following <u>factors</u> are important to your product — so you can select a fabric which has <u>the right properties</u>.

EXAM TIP:
To assess the suitability of a fabric you need to think about how it's <u>constructed</u> as well as about the <u>fibres</u>.

WARMTH

1) This is important in garments designed to <u>keep you warm</u>, e.g. a jumper.

2) Use fibres which are good <u>insulators</u> of heat, e.g. <u>wool</u> or <u>acrylic</u>.

3) <u>Knitted</u> fabrics are good insulators — air trapped in the loops keeps you warm.

APPEARANCE

1) <u>Appearance</u> can be important in making your product fit for purpose.

2) You might want to use a fabric that <u>drapes</u> well — e.g. <u>viscose</u> or <u>silk</u>. Or to make it look <u>smooth</u> and <u>shiny</u> choose a <u>satin weave</u>.

AFTER CARE

1) Some <u>products</u> will need <u>washing</u> regularly, e.g. children's clothing. So you need to make the after care an <u>easy</u> process.

2) Use <u>machine-washable</u> fibres (<u>cotton</u> can be washed at high temperatures) and fibres that <u>dry quickly</u> and <u>resist creasing</u>, e.g. <u>polyester</u>.

3) A <u>plain woven</u> fabric would be strong and <u>unlikely to shrink</u>, but a <u>knitted</u> fabric would <u>resist creasing</u>.

WEARABILITY AND COMFORT

1) <u>Everyday</u> clothes should be <u>comfortable</u> to wear.

2) This might mean using fibres which are:
<u>Soft</u> — like <u>cotton</u> and <u>viscose</u>.
<u>Breathable</u> — <u>absorbent</u> natural and regenerated fibres.
<u>Stretchy</u> — mix in <u>synthetic</u> fibres to add elasticity.

3) You could use a <u>warp-knitted</u> fabric — it will <u>stretch</u> but keep its shape.

DURABILITY

1) Many <u>clothes</u> need to be <u>durable</u>, e.g. children's wear and sports and outdoor clothes. It's also an important property for <u>functional</u> products, e.g. <u>rucksacks</u>.

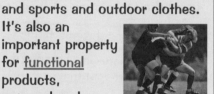

2) Use <u>strong</u>, <u>hard-wearing</u> fibres, like cotton, polyester or nylon.

3) Use a <u>plain or twill weave</u> for <u>strength</u>. Denim (twill-weave cotton) is ideal for kids' clothes.

Wire wool was an uncomfortable mistake...

SAFETY AND FLAMMABILITY

1) Certain textile products need to be <u>fire resistant</u> by <u>law</u>, e.g. upholstery (see p. 47).

2) It's important for some <u>garments</u> to have <u>low flammability</u>, e.g. night clothes. 100% <u>polyester</u> is a suitable fabric.

3) Some things should be made from a <u>flame proof</u> fabric such as <u>Nomex</u>®, e.g. firefighters' clothing.

4) More flammable fabrics can be given <u>flame retardant finishes</u> (see p. 40).

STAIN RESISTANCE

1) This is important in textile products that <u>can't</u> be <u>washed easily</u>, e.g. <u>carpets</u> and <u>upholstery</u>.

2) <u>Absorbent</u> fabrics <u>stain more easily</u>, so should be avoided. Use <u>woven fabrics</u> as these can be <u>scrubbed clean</u>.

3) Fabrics which stain easily can be given a <u>stain resistant finish</u> (see p. 40).

Jim the porpoise swam 900 miles — he was fit for a porpoise...

It must have been easier back in caveman times — "well you've got fur, or leaves... leaves have good stain resistance but aren't comfy or durable, so we'll use fur — it's soft, warm, and <u>very</u> 6752 BC."

Choosing Fabrics

The Fabric Specification Helps to Select a Fabric

A <u>fabric specification</u> is a <u>list</u> of <u>criteria</u> that the <u>fabric</u> for a particular product must <u>meet</u>.

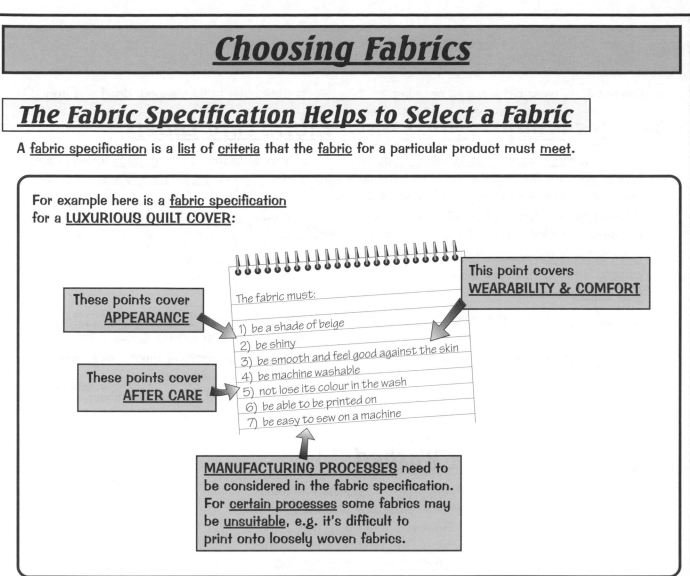

For example here is a <u>fabric specification</u>
for a <u>LUXURIOUS QUILT COVER</u>:

These points cover
APPEARANCE

These points cover
AFTER CARE

This point covers
WEARABILITY & COMFORT

The fabric must:
1) be a shade of beige
2) be shiny
3) be smooth and feel good against the skin
4) be machine washable
5) not lose its colour in the wash
6) be able to be printed on
7) be easy to sew on a machine

MANUFACTURING PROCESSES need to
be considered in the fabric specification.
For <u>certain processes</u> some fabrics may
be <u>unsuitable</u>, e.g. it's difficult to
print onto loosely woven fabrics.

Another factor to consider is <u>cost</u> — this will need to be <u>balanced</u> against the <u>suitability</u> of the fabric.

<u>Manufacturers</u> often have some input into the <u>fabric specification</u> — they'll use their <u>knowledge</u> of products and manufacturing processes to <u>specify criteria</u> for the fabric that a designer might miss.

Practice Questions

1) Define "fit for purpose".

2) Suggest the most <u>important property</u>, and a suitable <u>fibre</u> and <u>fabric construction</u> for:
   a) a mountain climber's hat
   b) a gardener's trousers
   c) a ball gown for wearing to a film premiere
   d) a baby's vest
   e) a bus seat cover

3) What is a <u>fabric specification</u>?

4) Suggest <u>two</u> points you would expect to find on the fabric specification for:
   a) a pair of oven gloves
   b) a builder's tool belt
   c) a baby's teddy bear
   d) a luxury robe/dressing gown

Fabric Maintenance

No one wants to wear dirty, soggy or crumpled things — textiles have to be <u>cleaned</u>, <u>dried</u> and <u>ironed</u>.

Textiles Products Must Have Fabric Care Labels

1) An <u>International Textile Care Labelling Code</u> (ITCLC) has been developed with <u>symbols</u> to tell people <u>how to care</u> for their textile products. The <u>care symbols</u> are used on <u>textile care labels</u>, washing machine programs and packets of washing powder.

2) A <u>care label</u> is a fabric label stitched onto a product. It includes the following information...

3) <u>Extra information</u> about a product might also be shown, either on the care label or on a separate label. E.g. <u>quality</u> marks.

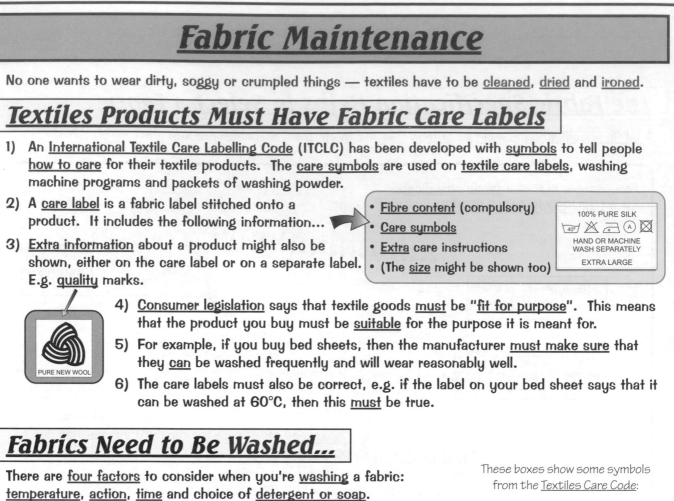

- <u>Fibre content</u> (compulsory)
- <u>Care symbols</u>
- <u>Extra</u> care instructions
- (The <u>size</u> might be shown too)

100% PURE SILK
HAND OR MACHINE WASH SEPARATELY
EXTRA LARGE

PURE NEW WOOL

4) <u>Consumer legislation</u> says that textile goods <u>must</u> be "<u>fit for purpose</u>". This means that the product you buy must be <u>suitable</u> for the purpose it is meant for.

5) For example, if you buy bed sheets, then the manufacturer <u>must make sure</u> that they <u>can</u> be washed frequently and will wear reasonably well.

6) The care labels must also be correct, e.g. if the label on your bed sheet says that it can be washed at 60°C, then this <u>must</u> be true.

Fabrics Need to Be Washed...

There are <u>four factors</u> to consider when you're <u>washing</u> a fabric: <u>temperature</u>, <u>action</u>, <u>time</u> and choice of <u>detergent or soap</u>.

1) <u>Heat</u> can help remove <u>stains</u>. However, under <u>very high</u> temperatures <u>viscose creases</u>, <u>wool felts</u> (shrinks and becomes matted like felt), and some <u>synthetic</u> fibres (e.g. polyester) permanently <u>change shape</u>. These fabrics need <u>lower</u> temperatures.

2) <u>Vigorous</u> washing can help remove <u>stains</u> too and long machine <u>spins</u> are good for removing <u>moisture</u>. Some fabrics, e.g. <u>linen</u>, stand up to <u>harsh movements</u>, but others are more delicate. E.g. <u>wool</u> may <u>felt</u>, so you need to use a <u>shorter spin</u>.

3) Delicate fabrics can also <u>stain</u> if they're in <u>water</u> for a <u>long time</u> — they may be given the <u>hand wash only</u> symbol.

4) <u>Strong detergents</u> get things <u>very clean</u>, but more <u>delicate</u> fabrics, like <u>silk</u>, need a <u>mild</u> detergent or soap.

5) Some <u>coloured</u> fabrics <u>mustn't be bleached</u>, or the colour will <u>change</u>. Coloured fabrics might also need to be washed <u>separately</u> in case the <u>dye comes out</u>.

These boxes show some symbols from the <u>Textiles Care Code</u>:

40°	Maximum temperature 40°
30°	Maximum temperature 30° Mild process
	Hand wash only
	Do not bleach
	Do not wash

...Dried...

1) Most things can be hung to dry on a <u>washing line</u>, but some <u>knitted</u> garments can <u>stretch</u>.

2) <u>Knitted</u> garments should be <u>reshaped</u> and laid out flat while <u>damp</u> so they maintain their <u>shape</u>.

3) Lots of clothes can be dried <u>quickly</u> in a <u>tumble drier</u> — but <u>wool</u>, <u>acrylic</u> and some <u>polyesters</u> will <u>shrink</u>, especially at <u>high temperatures</u>.

O	Tumble dry beneficial
	Do not tumble dry

I found this under my armpit:

When you leave home and have to do all your own <u>washing</u>, you'll be glad that you studied this page. <u>Shrinking</u> your pricey pure lamb's wool sweater to the size of a doll's jumper isn't really funny.

Section Two — Materials and Components

Fabric Maintenance

...And Ironed

Ironing <u>removes creases</u>. You need to use the <u>right temperature</u> — <u>too hot</u> and you could <u>melt</u>, <u>burn</u> or <u>shrink</u> the fabric.

1) A <u>hot</u> iron (3 dots) is great for <u>cotton</u> and <u>linen</u>. They're easier to iron when damp — so <u>steam</u> irons work best.

2) A <u>medium</u> iron (2 dots) works well for most <u>mixed fabrics</u>, but <u>not</u> for some <u>synthetics</u> which could <u>melt</u>.
A <u>cool</u> iron (1 dot) is good for these and other fibres like <u>silk</u>.

3) Textured fabrics like <u>seersucker</u> mustn't be ironed, because ironing can <u>remove</u> the <u>texture</u>.

⌧	Cool iron
⌧	Warm iron
⌧	Hot iron
⌧	Do not iron

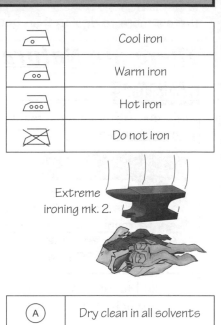

Extreme ironing mk. 2.

Some Fabrics Are Dry-Clean Only

1) Some garments and soft furnishings must be <u>dry-cleaned</u>, so that the fibres don't <u>absorb moisture</u> and <u>lose</u> their <u>shape</u>.

2) Chemicals (called <u>solvents</u>) are used to clean instead of <u>water</u>. Solvents are much better at removing <u>grease and oil</u> than water is.

3) Dry cleaning's used for <u>tailored</u> garments like <u>jackets</u> to make sure the different interfacings don't <u>shrink differently</u> and cause the garment to <u>lose its shape</u>.

4) Dry cleaning's <u>expensive</u>, but things come back looking <u>like new</u>. For <u>big</u> and <u>heavy</u> items like a <u>winter coat</u> or <u>curtains</u>, it's much easier to get the <u>professionals</u> to clean them.

Ⓐ	Dry clean in all solvents
⌧	Do not dry clean

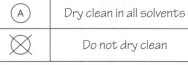

Consider Fabric Maintenance in Your Designs

When choosing a <u>fabric</u> for a <u>textile product</u>, you need to think about how <u>its purpose</u> affects the <u>maintenance</u> requirements of the fabric.

EXAMPLE: TROUSERS FOR TODDLERS

Young children are likely to <u>fall over</u> a lot and <u>crawl</u> on the ground so the fabric will get <u>very dirty</u>. So as well as the fabric being <u>hard-wearing</u>, it needs to be:

1) Able to be <u>washed</u> at a <u>high temperature</u> with <u>detergent</u> — to get things like grass stains out. ➡ <u>Cotton</u> or <u>linen</u> would be good

2) Cotton <u>dries more quickly</u> than linen, so <u>cotton</u> would be a better choice.

And when you've chosen your fabrics you'll need to make sure the <u>right care symbols</u> go on the <u>label</u>, so people who buy the product know how to <u>maintain it properly</u>.

Practice Questions

1) What information is it <u>compulsory</u> to show on a garment's <u>care label</u>?

2) Give <u>an example</u> of:
   a) a fibre that can't be washed vigorously at high temperatures.
   b) a fibre that stands up well to hot, vigorous washing.

3) How should <u>knitted</u> garments be dried? Why is this?

4) Why must you make sure that your iron is the <u>correct temperature</u> before ironing a fabric?

5) Explain why some garments must be <u>dry-cleaned</u> rather than washed conventionally?

Dyeing

There's more to dyeing than you might think — tea and onions, for example...

There are Natural Dyes and Chemical Dyes

Natural Dyes

Until the 1850s all dyes came from natural sources...

They're made from things like onions, beetroot, tea, raspberries or flowers etc.

Chemical dyes

These were invented in the 1850s.
ADVANTAGES:
- Colours are brighter.
- Easier and cheaper to make.
- Exactly the same colour can be achieved repeatedly.

DISADVANTAGE:
Some are toxic — they can be harmful to people and the environment (see pages 44-45).

Fibres and fabrics can be dyed at different stages of the manufacturing process — individual fibres, yarns or whole pieces of fabric can all be dyed. The methods here are for dyeing fabrics.

Some Fabrics are Better for Dyeing than Others

1) Natural fibres (like cotton, wool and silk) are the best for dyeing as they're very absorbent.

2) The colour of the fabric you begin with makes a difference to the final colour — for example if you dye white fabric red, you get red fabric — if you dye yellow fabric red, you get orange.

3) Fabrics that have an uneven colour need to be bleached before dyeing to ensure an even colour.

4) For some fabrics and dyes you need to use a chemical called a mordant (e.g. salt) to fix the colour to the fabric. This makes the fabric colour fast — the dye won't come out in the wash.

Batch Dyeing is a Commercial Dyeing Technique

1) Commercial dyeing involves dyeing a huge amount of fabric at a time. The fabric is dyed a uniform colour. It can be done continuously — this is where very long lengths of fabric are dyed the same colour in a continuous process. Or it can be done in batches...

2) In batch dyeing, a batch of fabric is dyed with one colour, then another batch with a different colour, and so on. Here's how it's done:

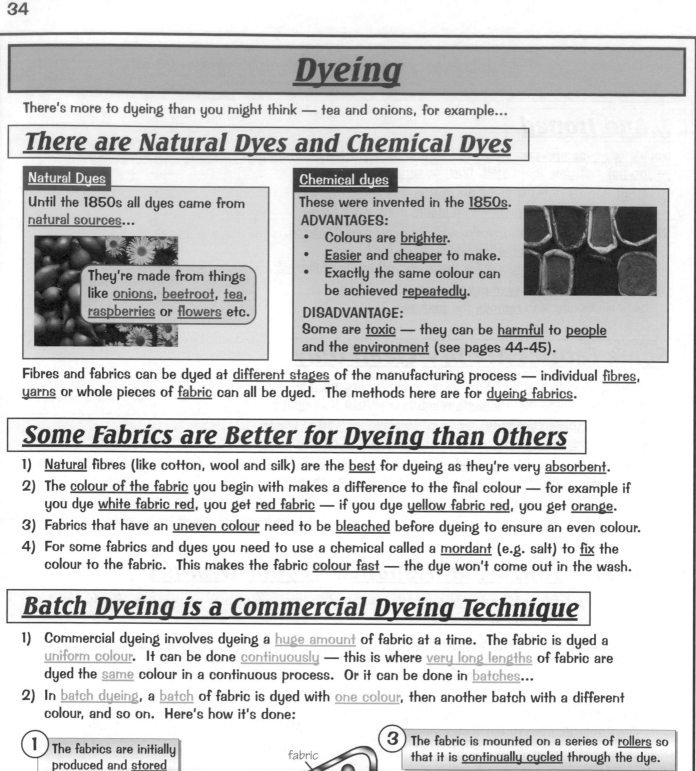

① The fabrics are initially produced and stored without dyeing.

② When a large amount of fabric of the same colour is required, it is dyed in a batch.

fabric

rollers

dye

③ The fabric is mounted on a series of rollers so that it is continually cycled through the dye.

④ The dyed material is put in a separate machine to fix the dye (to stop it from running).

Colours can go out of fashion quickly.

3) Batch dyeing is useful because as fashionable colours change quickly, textiles manufacturers need to be able to respond quickly, and produce large batches of fabrics in different colours.

Finished this page alive — you'll live to dye another day...

Dyeing with onions, eh... last night I discovered a new natural dye, it gives a nice bright orange colour, and I applied it in no time at all by just slopping it on my shirt — I think I'll call it prawn vindaloo...

Dyeing

Hand Dyeing — Use a Resist to Make Patterns...

One of the <u>advantages</u> of <u>hand</u> dyeing is that you can add <u>designs</u> to the fabric using a 'resist'. A '<u>resist</u>' is something which <u>prevents the dye</u> from reaching the <u>fabric</u> — it's applied in a pattern before dyeing.

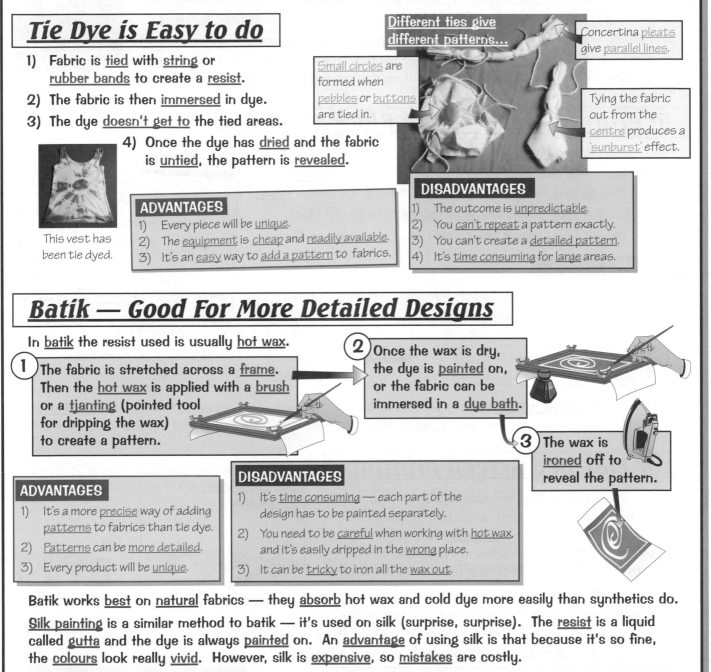

Tie Dye is Easy to do

1) Fabric is <u>tied</u> with <u>string</u> or <u>rubber bands</u> to create a <u>resist</u>.

2) The fabric is then <u>immersed</u> in dye.

3) The dye <u>doesn't get to</u> the tied areas.

4) Once the dye has <u>dried</u> and the fabric is <u>untied</u>, the pattern is <u>revealed</u>.

This vest has been tie dyed.

Different ties give different patterns...

Concertina <u>pleats</u> give <u>parallel lines</u>.

<u>Small circles</u> are formed when <u>pebbles</u> or <u>buttons</u> are tied in.

Tying the fabric out from the <u>centre</u> produces a '<u>sunburst</u>' effect.

ADVANTAGES
1) Every piece will be <u>unique</u>.
2) The <u>equipment</u> is <u>cheap</u> and <u>readily available</u>.
3) It's an <u>easy</u> way to <u>add a pattern</u> to fabrics.

DISADVANTAGES
1) The outcome is <u>unpredictable</u>.
2) You <u>can't repeat</u> a pattern exactly.
3) You can't create a <u>detailed pattern</u>.
4) It's <u>time consuming</u> for <u>large</u> areas.

Batik — Good For More Detailed Designs

In <u>batik</u> the resist used is usually <u>hot wax</u>.

1 The fabric is stretched across a <u>frame</u>. Then the <u>hot wax</u> is applied with a <u>brush</u> or a <u>tjanting</u> (pointed tool for dripping the wax) to create a pattern.

2 Once the wax is dry, the dye is <u>painted</u> on, or the fabric can be immersed in a <u>dye bath</u>.

3 The wax is <u>ironed</u> off to reveal the pattern.

ADVANTAGES
1) It's a more <u>precise</u> way of adding <u>patterns</u> to fabrics than tie dye.
2) <u>Patterns</u> can be <u>more detailed</u>.
3) Every product will be <u>unique</u>.

DISADVANTAGES
1) It's <u>time consuming</u> — each part of the design has to be painted separately.
2) You need to be <u>careful</u> when working with <u>hot wax</u>, and it's easily dripped in the <u>wrong</u> place.
3) It can be <u>tricky</u> to iron all the <u>wax out</u>.

Batik works <u>best</u> on <u>natural</u> fabrics — they <u>absorb</u> hot wax and cold dye more easily than synthetics do.

<u>Silk painting</u> is a similar method to batik — it's used on silk (surprise, surprise). The <u>resist</u> is a liquid called <u>gutta</u> and the dye is always <u>painted</u> on. An <u>advantage</u> of using silk is that because it's so fine, the <u>colours</u> look really <u>vivid</u>. However, silk is <u>expensive</u>, so <u>mistakes</u> are costly.

Practice Questions

1) What are the <u>advantages</u> of using <u>chemical dyes</u> over natural ones?

2) In the dyeing process, explain why a fabric might need to be:
   a) <u>bleached</u>
   b) treated with a <u>mordant</u>

3) James is trying to dye a star and turtle pattern onto some <u>polyester</u> fabric.
   a) Suggest a suitable method of <u>hand dyeing</u> he could use.
   b) Explain how James could produce <u>better</u> results by using a <u>different</u> fabric.

Printing

Just like with dyeing, you need to know methods of printing that you can do by hand, as well as those that are used commercially. Lots to learn. Here we go...

Printing is Used to Apply a Design to Fabric

1) Printing is the process of applying ink, dye or paint to fabric in defined patterns.
2) Printing can be done in small quantities by hand, or in large quantities commercially.
3) Materials with a tight weave are best for printing on because they have a smooth surface for the dye to be applied to and no surface pattern to detract from the design.

Some printed clothes

To Print by Hand — Use Block Printing...

You need a printing block with a raised design.

1) You can make one by drawing a pattern on a piece of wood and then cutting the background away, leaving the design raised.
2) Or you can stick pieces of card or string onto a solid block.
3) You can also buy rubber blocks with designs already on them.

The printing process...

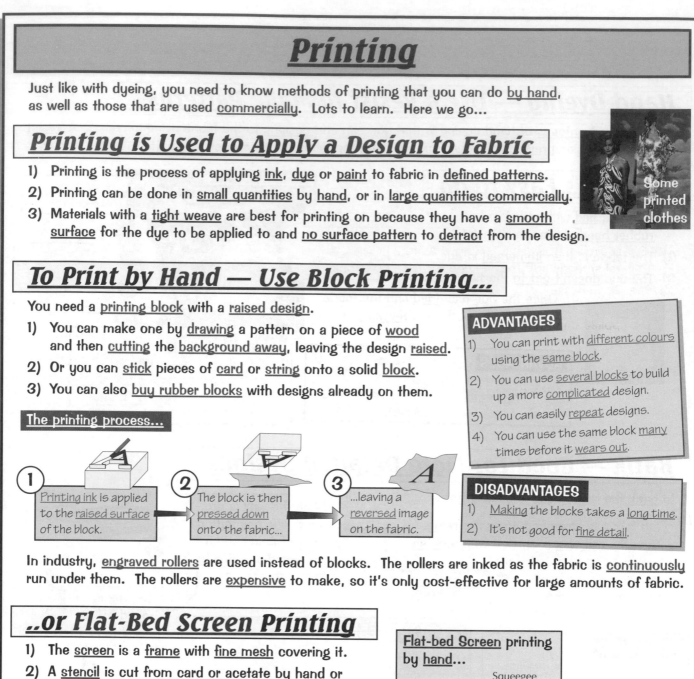

① Printing ink is applied to the raised surface of the block.

② The block is then pressed down onto the fabric...

③ ...leaving a reversed image on the fabric.

ADVANTAGES
1) You can print with different colours using the same block.
2) You can use several blocks to build up a more complicated design.
3) You can easily repeat designs.
4) You can use the same block many times before it wears out.

DISADVANTAGES
1) Making the blocks takes a long time.
2) It's not good for fine detail.

In industry, engraved rollers are used instead of blocks. The rollers are inked as the fabric is continuously run under them. The rollers are expensive to make, so it's only cost-effective for large amounts of fabric.

..or Flat-Bed Screen Printing

1) The screen is a frame with fine mesh covering it.
2) A stencil is cut from card or acetate by hand or using CAD/CAM and put beneath the screen (on top of the fabric). Alternatively, parts of the screen itself can be blocked off to create the design.
3) Printing ink is poured onto the screen.
4) A squeegee is pressed down and drawn across the screen, forcing the ink through the mesh and the holes in the stencil.
5) The screen is lifted up and the design is left on the fabric.

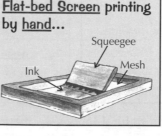

Flat-bed Screen printing by hand...

Squeegee

Ink

Mesh

The Squee Gees

ADVANTAGES
1) Can produce intricate patterns that can be repeated accurately.
2) Good for printing large areas of colour.
3) Easy to use many colours — by using several screens.
4) Printing is quick to do (once you have the screens/stencils).

DISADVANTAGES
1) Making the screens/stencils takes a long time.
2) Each colour has to be applied separately.

Printing sending you to sleep — go and find a flat-bed...

Printing — reading about it is about as exciting as watching ink dry. Anyway, just learn how to do it and remember that you can do flat-bed screen printing by hand, but it's also done on a larger scale...

Printing

Screen Printing is Done Commercially with Machines

1) Commercial screen printing uses <u>machines</u> to repeat the <u>same pattern</u> all the way along a <u>long length</u> of fabric.

2) There are <u>two</u> methods of commercial screen printing. Like screen printing by hand, they both use some sort of <u>screen</u> and a <u>squeegee</u>.

> Remember — the screens can be made using CAD and CAM.

Commercial flat-bed screen printing

1) This is similar to flat-bed screen printing <u>by hand</u>. <u>Several</u> screens are used — one for <u>each</u> colour.

2) The fabric passes <u>under</u> the screens on a <u>conveyor belt</u> and the colours are applied one after the other.

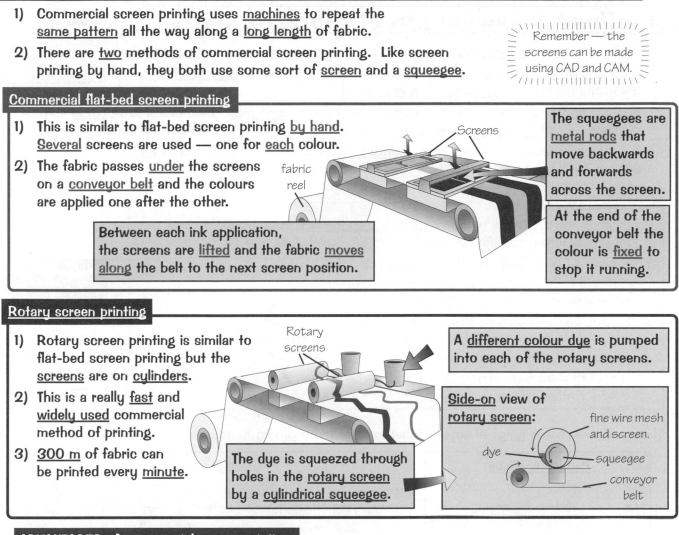

Screens

fabric reel

The squeegees are <u>metal rods</u> that move backwards and forwards across the screen.

Between each ink application, the screens are <u>lifted</u> and the fabric <u>moves along</u> the belt to the next screen position.

At the end of the conveyor belt the colour is <u>fixed</u> to stop it running.

Rotary screen printing

1) Rotary screen printing is similar to flat-bed screen printing but the <u>screens</u> are on <u>cylinders</u>.

2) This is a really <u>fast</u> and <u>widely used</u> commercial method of printing.

3) <u>300 m</u> of fabric can be printed every <u>minute</u>.

Rotary screens

A <u>different colour dye</u> is pumped into each of the rotary screens.

The dye is squeezed through holes in the <u>rotary screen</u> by a <u>cylindrical squeegee</u>.

<u>Side-on</u> view of <u>rotary screen</u>:

fine wire mesh and screen.

dye

squeegee

conveyor belt

ADVANTAGES of commercial screen printing:

1) Just as with <u>hand</u> screen printing, <u>intricate patterns</u> using <u>many colours</u> can be <u>repeated</u> accurately.

2) The <u>machinery</u> makes the printing process <u>much quicker</u> and <u>large amounts</u> of fabric can be printed at once. Rotary printing is the <u>quickest</u> way — as fabric is passed along the conveyor belt <u>continuously</u>.

3) The <u>screen making</u> process can be <u>computer-controlled</u>, which makes it much <u>quicker</u>.

DISADVANTAGES of commercial screen printing:

1) Setting up commercial <u>machinery</u> is <u>expensive</u>.

2) <u>Screen making</u> takes a <u>long time</u>, unless it's done using CAD/CAM.

Practice Questions

1) Explain why <u>tightly woven</u> fabrics are best for printing on.

2) Maurice wants to produce bags with a <u>handmade</u> appearance, featuring a <u>simple</u> printed design.
   a) Suggest a <u>printing method</u> he could use.
   b) Give <u>one advantage</u> and <u>one disadvantage</u> of this printing method.

3) Robin is printing fabric for football quilt covers with a "<u>You've Scored</u>" design repeated over and over on it.
   a) Describe how <u>commercial flat-bed</u> screen printing could be used to apply the design.
   b) What are the <u>disadvantages</u> of using this method?

Decoration and Enhancement

Bored with the same old plain, bland, oven gloves...well now it's time to turn up the heat — textile products (including oven gloves) can be made more interesting with a <u>surface embellishment</u> (decoration).

Appliqué is Sewing Bits of Fabric On Top

1) Appliqué involves <u>cutting shapes</u> out of fabric and <u>sewing</u> them onto a <u>textile product</u>.

2) It adds <u>texture</u> and <u>colour</u> to a product, and it can be applied to <u>large areas</u>. It's useful for creating <u>pictures</u> and <u>patterns</u>.

3) <u>Non-woven</u> fabrics, such as felt, are often used as they <u>don't fray</u>. They can also be <u>cut in any direction</u> — so <u>more shapes</u> can be cut from a single piece of fabric, which keeps costs down.

4) It's a popular technique for decorating <u>children's</u> products, as it can be made <u>soft</u> to touch and without <u>small pieces</u> that could be unsafe for children.

HERE'S HOW TO DO IT:

1) <u>Position</u> the cut shape on the fabric and <u>keep in place</u> using pins, tacking stitches, or a fusible interface like bondaweb (see p. 43).

2) The use of <u>bondaweb</u> can also add <u>bulk</u>, stop the appliqué from <u>stretching</u> when it's being <u>sewn</u> and prevent woven fabric from <u>fraying</u>.

3) <u>Fraying</u> can also be prevented by <u>folding</u> the edges of the shape under before stitching.

4) Machine stitch the design. A <u>close zigzag</u> stitch is usually used — or <u>different stitches</u> can be used for other effects.

Bottom fabric
Top fabric

<u>Coloured thread</u> or sequins and beads can also be used for added <u>decorative</u> effect.

There are some other <u>types</u> of appliqué that can add more <u>variety</u> to your designs...

Padded appliqué

Top fabric
Wadding
Bottom fabric

1) Appliqué can be <u>padded</u> by placing <u>wadding</u> or <u>stuffing</u> between the fabric pieces.

2) This creates a <u>3D effect</u> and gives <u>depth</u>.

Reverse appliqué

1) This is when <u>holes</u> are cut out of the <u>main fabric</u> and the appliqué is sewn on <u>behind</u> the hole on the <u>inside</u> of the product.

Top fabric
Bottom fabric
Hem folded under

2) The hole has to be cut <u>slightly smaller</u> than you want it to <u>end up</u> to allow for a <u>hem</u> to stop the <u>material</u> from <u>fraying</u>.

ADVANTAGES OF APPLIQUÉ

1) It <u>strengthens</u> the base fabric because it makes a <u>double layer</u>.

2) <u>Shapes</u> can be <u>repeated accurately</u> if templates are used.

3) It allows <u>scraps</u> of fabric to be <u>used</u> rather than being wasted.

4) It can be used to add <u>colour and texture</u> to <u>large areas</u>.

5) It can be sewn <u>automatically</u> using CAM machines.

DISADVANTAGES

1) It requires a lot of <u>extra material</u>.

2) It adds <u>thickness</u> and <u>weight</u> to products.

Whoops...I forgot to sew on the reverse appliqué...

Appliqué — a bit patchy when it comes to comedy material...

You can incorporate the different techniques on these pages in your designs to spice them up — but you also need to learn the <u>advantages</u> and <u>disadvantages</u> of each different technique...

Decoration and Enhancement

Quilting Also Uses Wadding

1) Quilting uses wadding between two layers of fabric which are then stitched together in straight lines or in a pattern.

2) Quilting is often used to give added warmth to a product (e.g. an anorak or bed cover). The wadding traps warm air between the layers of fabric.

Top fabric
Bottom fabric
Wadding

ADVANTAGE
Can create interesting 3D effects and warmth.

DISADVANTAGES
1) Requires a lot of material.
2) Time consuming.

Embroidery is Decorative Stitching

1) Embroidery is decorative stitching — it can be done by hand or machine.

2) Different types of thread give different textures and finishes, e.g. silk will give a shiny finish.

3) Lots of different stitches can be used.

4) CAM embroidery machines can be used to automatically produce designs.

Examples of Embroidery Stitches
Chain stitch
Herringbone stitch
Blanket stitch

An embroidered design

Fabric can be stretched across an embroidery hoop or frame to make sure the stitching is even.

ADVANTAGES
1) Can do very intricate patterns.
2) Adds texture as well as colour.
2) Hand embroidery gives unique results.
3) Quick to do by machine — can be done automatically using CAD/CAM.

DISADVANTAGES
1) Can be easily damaged so it's more difficult to care for.
2) Very time consuming and expensive if done by hand.
3) Hand embroidered products won't be identical.

Use Beads and Sequins and Combine the Techniques

Beads and sequins can be sewn on by hand to add decoration...

They also reflect light in interesting ways.

They add colour, and texture.

..you can also buy sequined material.

Remember you can combine the different techniques on these pages in your designs to really mix it up...

Practice Questions

1) a) Name the technique used to apply this flower decoration.
   b) Suggest two ways to prevent the decoration from fraying.

2) Here's a diagram showing a cross-section through some quilting.
   a-d) Name the parts labelled a-d.
   e) What main property does quilting add to a fabric?

3) a) What is the main purpose of embroidery?
   b) Give one disadvantage of using embroidery to decorate a product.

Fabric Finishes

Without finishes the world would be a mess — we'd all be creased, stained, soaking wet and some of us would be on fire. Finishes can be applied <u>chemically</u> or <u>mechanically</u>...

Finishes Improve The Performance of Fabrics

There are four <u>reasons</u> why finishes are used. They're all to do with <u>changing</u> something about the fabric.

1) To change the <u>APPEARANCE</u> of the fabric (e.g. sheen and colour).

2) To change the fabric's <u>TEXTURE</u> (e.g. smoothness and softness).

3) To change <u>WEARING PROPERTIES</u> (e.g. crease resistance, stain resistance).

4) To change <u>AFTER CARE CHARACTERISTICS</u> (e.g. shrinking).

Finishes are usually the <u>last stage</u> of fabric processing.

Some Finishing is Done Using Chemicals

<u>Chemicals</u> are applied to <u>fibres</u> or <u>fabrics</u> during manufacture to give fabrics beneficial properties.

FLAME RETARDANCE

1) <u>Flame retardant</u> finishes are chemicals that make fabrics <u>less likely to catch fire</u>.

2) They're often used on <u>flammable</u> fibres like <u>cotton</u>. Products they're used on include workwear for <u>welders</u>, <u>racing drivers'</u> overalls, <u>night</u> clothes and fabric for <u>soft furnishings</u> — to make them meet fire safety requirements (see p. 47).

3) Using a fire retardant finish on fabrics like cotton makes the fabric <u>slightly stiffer</u>, but the fabric is still <u>softer</u> and <u>cheaper to produce</u> than a synthetic flameproof fabric like Nomex® (see p. 28). However, specially produced fabrics like Nomex® do provide <u>better protection</u>.

4) Some flame retardant finishes can be <u>washed out</u>, so care is needed when washing.

WATER RESISTANCE

1) Chemicals (e.g. <u>silicones</u>) can be applied to the surface of fabrics to <u>stop water droplets</u> passing through.

The water forms <u>beads</u> on the surface.

2) These finishes <u>don't</u> make the fabric <u>waterproof</u> — if the surface becomes <u>saturated</u> (completely covered in water) the water will <u>leak</u> through.

3) Fabrics with a water resistant finish can be <u>washed</u> and <u>dry-cleaned</u> without affecting the performance of the finish.

4) <u>Nylon</u> is often given a <u>water resistant</u> finish and used to make <u>coats</u> and <u>tents</u>.

STAIN RESISTANCE

1) Fabrics can be made stain resistant with a finish of a mixture of <u>silicone</u> and <u>fluorine</u> or a <u>Teflon®</u> <u>coating</u> (this is also used on nonstick frying pans).

2) These finishes stop <u>grease</u> and <u>dirt</u> from <u>penetrating</u> the fabric.

3) Stain resistant finishes are used a lot on <u>carpets</u> and <u>upholstery</u>.

4) More recently, <u>nanoparticles</u> have been used to give improved <u>stain resistance</u> (see p. 29).

Fabric finish — is that the end of a sack race...

So you've finished this page — well done. You've learnt three finishes so far, just six to go. When you're thinking about adding a finish, you need to <u>balance</u> the potential effects with the costs involved.

Fabric Finishes

A few more chemical finishes and then we'll <u>finish off</u> with some mechanical finishes.

1) **SHRINK RESISTANT** finishes are applied to <u>fabrics</u> such as wool, which are prone to <u>shrinking</u> when <u>machine washed</u>.

2) <u>Scales</u> on wool fibres cause wool to shrink in the wash. <u>Hot water</u> and <u>rubbing</u> cause the fibres to <u>move</u> against each other and the <u>scales</u> tangle and lock together.

3) To stop this, the <u>scales</u> can be <u>permanently removed</u> with <u>chlorine</u>, or a <u>coating</u> applied to <u>smooth</u> the surface of the fibres.

1) **CREASE RESISTANT** finishes are given to fabrics that <u>crease easily</u> (e.g. <u>cotton</u> and <u>linen</u>).

2) The <u>chemicals</u> or <u>resins</u> used can make fabrics feel slightly <u>stiffer</u>.

3) The finish is <u>durable</u>, but <u>care</u> is needed when <u>washing</u> and <u>ironing</u>.

1) **THERMOCHROMIC DYES** change from <u>one colour</u> to <u>another</u> when the <u>temperature changes</u>.

2) They can be <u>printed</u> onto fabrics to give a <u>smart finish</u> — one that <u>responds</u> to <u>changes</u> in its <u>surroundings</u>.

3) This finish doesn't tend to be very <u>durable</u>.

Some Finishes are Applied Mechanically

The following are mechanical finishes — <u>machines</u> are used to create them. Mechanical finishes are <u>cheaper</u> to apply than chemical finishes, so won't increase the <u>cost of the product</u> too much.

Fabric brushing

1) Brushing fabric gives it a <u>soft, raised</u> surface.

2) Fabrics can be <u>brushed</u> by passing them between rollers covered with wire brushes to raise the surface.

3) The raised surface <u>traps air</u> and keeps the body warmer.

4) Brushing is a <u>permanent</u> finish.

Textiles for <u>babies</u> are often brushed for <u>softness</u> and insulation.

Calendering

1) Calendering makes fabrics *smoother* and <u>shinier</u>.

2) <u>Heavy heated rollers</u> are used to <u>squash</u> the fabric.

3) The finish is <u>not permanent</u> and <u>wears off</u> with time, but it's fairly <u>durable</u>.

Pre-shrinkage

1) <u>Natural fibres</u> which are prone to <u>shrinking</u> (e.g. wool and cotton) can be <u>pre-shrunk</u>.

2) This <u>reduces</u> further <u>shrinkage</u> when the fabrics are washed.

3) It's done by <u>steaming</u> the fabric on a <u>vibrating</u> conveyor belt.

Don't worry — we all get caught out by shrinkage...

Practice Questions

1) What are the <u>four main reasons</u> for applying a finish to a fabric?

2) Fred's overalls have a <u>flame retardant</u> finish.
   Why is it important that he follows the washing instructions carefully?

3) How can treatment with chlorine <u>prevent</u> a garment made from <u>wool</u> from <u>shrinking</u>?

4) a) What are <u>mechanical</u> finishes?
   b) Give an <u>advantage</u> of using a mechanical finish rather than a chemical one.

Manufactured Components

Unless your project is to make a flannel or a bed sheet, you're gonna need to use some components.

Components are Pre-manufactured Parts

1) Components are the bits and pieces that you use in <u>addition</u> to the fabric to make a <u>textile product</u>.

2) They can be <u>functional</u>, e.g. a zip to close your coat, or <u>decorative</u>, e.g. a lace edging.

Some Components are Fastenings

Fastenings are used to <u>close</u> products, or parts of products (like pockets). They need to be <u>suitable</u> for the <u>product</u> and intended <u>user</u>.

There's more on choosing <u>safe</u> components on pages 46-47 in Section Three.

Zips

1) They can be made out of <u>plastic</u> or <u>metal</u>, and be <u>big</u> and <u>bulky</u> or <u>small</u> and <u>concealed</u> (hidden) in your textile design.

2) Some zips are <u>fixed</u> at <u>one end</u> (e.g. on handbags). Zips on <u>jackets</u> are <u>not fixed</u> (so you can get the jacket off).

3) Zips with <u>two sliders</u> can be opened in two directions — the ends can be fixed (e.g. on suitcases) or open (e.g. on some jackets).

ADVANTAGES OF ZIPS

1) They're a <u>secure</u> fastening — they close the product fully with no gaps.

2) They're <u>quick</u> and <u>simple</u> to attach.

3) They <u>lay flat</u> and don't add <u>bulk</u>.

4) They're <u>hard-wearing</u> and can be <u>washed</u>.

5) Colours can <u>match</u> or <u>contrast</u> with the fabric.

DISADVANTAGES OF ZIPS

1) They can <u>snag</u> delicate fabrics.

2) They don't add any <u>interest</u> to products.

3) They're difficult to <u>replace</u>.

Toggles and Buttons

These are sewn on and require a <u>buttonhole</u> or a <u>loop</u> to fasten to.

They can be made of <u>any hard</u> material — <u>plastic</u>, <u>metal</u>, <u>wood</u>, and even <u>glass</u>.

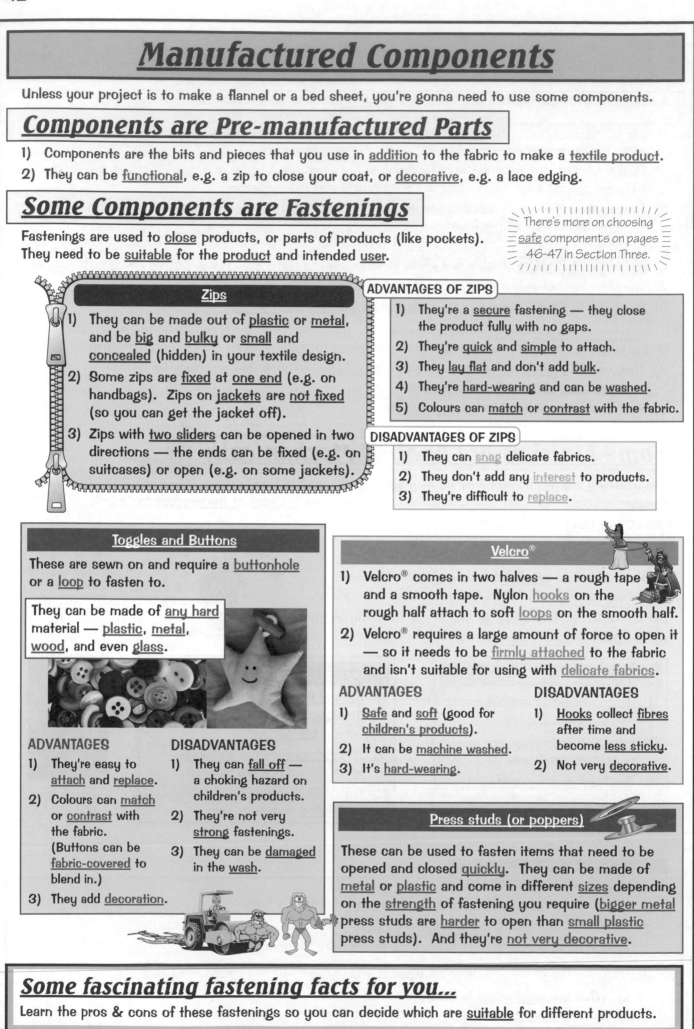

ADVANTAGES

1) They're easy to <u>attach</u> and <u>replace</u>.

2) Colours can <u>match</u> or <u>contrast</u> with the fabric. (Buttons can be <u>fabric-covered</u> to blend in.)

3) They add <u>decoration</u>.

DISADVANTAGES

1) They can <u>fall off</u> — a choking hazard on children's products.

2) They're not very <u>strong</u> fastenings.

3) They can be <u>damaged</u> in the <u>wash</u>.

Velcro®

1) Velcro® comes in two halves — a rough tape and a smooth tape. Nylon <u>hooks</u> on the rough half attach to soft <u>loops</u> on the smooth half.

2) Velcro® requires a large amount of force to open it — so it needs to be <u>firmly attached</u> to the fabric and isn't suitable for using with <u>delicate fabrics</u>.

ADVANTAGES

1) <u>Safe</u> and <u>soft</u> (good for <u>children's products</u>).

2) It can be <u>machine washed</u>.

3) It's <u>hard-wearing</u>.

DISADVANTAGES

1) <u>Hooks</u> collect <u>fibres</u> after time and become <u>less sticky</u>.

2) Not very <u>decorative</u>.

Press studs (or poppers)

These can be used to fasten items that need to be opened and closed <u>quickly</u>. They can be made of <u>metal</u> or <u>plastic</u> and come in different <u>sizes</u> depending on the <u>strength</u> of fastening you require (<u>bigger metal</u> press studs are <u>harder</u> to open than <u>small plastic</u> press studs). And they're <u>not very decorative</u>.

Some fascinating fastening facts for you...

Learn the pros & cons of these fastenings so you can decide which are <u>suitable</u> for different products.

Manufactured Components

You Can Use Other Components in Your Designs

1) **THREADS** can be used for joining fabric, securing other components or decorative stitching (see p. 39).

2) They come in different thicknesses and textures. Sewing threads are fine and will form neat and strong seams. Embroidery threads can be thicker and have a variety of textures.

1) **TRIMMINGS** include lace, ribbons, braid, laces, beads and sequins.

2) They're mainly used to add decoration.

3) Ribbons, braids and laces can also be threaded through eyelets or holes to make a fastening. But they're often not very secure.

1) **INTERFACINGS** are extra layers of fabric hidden inside a product. They're used to give strength, stability and support. They come in different weights for different uses.

2) They're used in collars, cuffs, around button holes, and anywhere a product needs extra strength.

3) Some interfacings are 'fusible' — they stick onto materials when heated (e.g. by ironing). Bondaweb is a fusible double-sided interfacing used to bind fabrics together. It's used, for example, in appliqué (see p. 38).

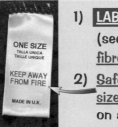

1) **LABELS** show care instructions (see pages 32-33) and the fibre content.

2) Safety information and size might also be shown on a label.

1) **ELECTRONIC COMPONENTS** can be added to textile products for decoration (e.g. LED lights in clothing) or for function (e.g. heated motorbike clothing).

2) Power for components can be supplied from batteries or solar panels that are integrated into the textile product.

MOTIFS are small fabric badges (often embroidered) that are sewn on to add decoration. They can be used to show membership of clubs or teams.

Technological Advances in Component Design...

1) Sensors in clothes that monitor things like heart rate and blood pressure.

2) Washable electronic switches to operate things like MP3 players and mobile phones.

3) Wadding that responds automatically to temperature so that it insulates when it's cold and doesn't insulate when it's hot is another idea.

4) The development of conductive fabrics (see p. 29) is making it easier to integrate electronic components into clothing as it means that wires aren't needed to conduct the electricity.

Practice Questions

1) Describe how zips are attached differently to a coat than to trousers.

2) How might Velcro® lose its effectiveness over time?

3) Alison is designing a cardigan that will be made using a delicate knitted fabric.
   a) Suggest a fastening suitable for use with this type of fabric.
   b) What are the disadvantages of this type of fastening?

4) Bondaweb is a fusible interfacing.
   a) What are interfacings and why are they used?
   b) What does it mean if an interfacing is 'fusible'?

Textiles and the Environment

Textiles production can cause lots of environmental problems. It's up to <u>designers and manufacturers</u> to <u>minimise</u> their environmental impact and <u>satisfy consumer demands</u> for more sustainable products.

The Textiles Industry Can Harm the Environment

Here are the main environmental <u>issues</u> and some ways the textiles industry can <u>reduce</u> its impact...

POLLUTION AND USE OF RESOURCES

Textiles production uses <u>lots</u> of <u>energy</u> — most is from <u>burning non-renewable</u> resources (e.g. coal, oil). This uses up <u>valuable</u> resources, <u>pollutes the air</u> and releases CO_2 — causing <u>global warming</u>.

Some <u>fabrics</u> are made from <u>non-renewable</u> resources, e.g. polyester is made from crude oil.

Manufacturing processes use a <u>lot of water</u>.

Use <u>energy</u> from <u>renewable</u> sources, e.g. <u>wind</u> power, and be more <u>energy efficient</u>, for example using <u>natural</u> instead of <u>electric light</u> if possible.

Use <u>fabrics</u> made from <u>biofibres</u> (see next page).

Use <u>water</u> more <u>efficiently</u>, e.g. <u>reuse</u> waste water in the <u>dyeing process</u>.

TRANSPORT POLLUTION

Textile factories are often in <u>different countries</u> from their products' markets, so a lot of <u>fuel</u> is <u>burned</u> in transporting products. <u>Raw materials</u> are also <u>transported</u> long distances.

Use <u>efficient distribution</u> methods (e.g. trains not lorries) and get raw materials from <u>local suppliers</u>.

PROBLEMS CAUSED BY COTTON FARMING

<u>Artificial</u> fertilisers and pesticides are used to increase crop yields. These <u>fertilisers</u> can <u>pollute rivers</u> and <u>harm wildlife</u>. <u>Pesticides</u> can <u>kill other creatures</u> (not just pests).

Use <u>organic cotton</u>, or other natural fibres grown organically (see next page).

DISPOSAL OF WASTE MATERIALS

Textile factories can generate a lot of <u>waste</u> fabric and other materials, e.g. packaging. This waste ends up in huge <u>landfill</u> sites and takes hundreds of years to <u>decompose</u>.

<u>Our old clothes</u> are thrown away and end up in <u>landfill</u> too.

RECYCLE TEXTILES like this...
- <u>Reuse</u> waste <u>material</u>, e.g. use <u>fabric cutoffs</u> in <u>new products</u>.
- <u>Break</u> waste <u>fabric</u> back <u>down</u> into <u>fibres</u> that can be <u>reused</u>, e.g. for insulation, or respun.
- <u>Recycle</u> our <u>old clothes</u> — the deconstructed parts can be used in <u>new products</u>, or give them to <u>charity</u> so they can be <u>reused</u>.

<u>Reduce waste</u>, e.g. by using less packaging.

Use <u>biodegradable fabrics</u> (see next page).

DISPOSAL OF TOXIC CHEMICALS

<u>Toxic chemicals</u> are used in dyeing and finishing processes (e.g. bleach, toxic dyes). These are contained in <u>waste water</u> that can end up in <u>streams</u> and <u>rivers</u>, and <u>poison wildlife</u>.

<u>Remove</u> chemicals <u>before</u> the water leaves the factory — the chemical sludge can then be disposed of properly.

Use <u>non-toxic</u> dyes (made from natural substances) and <u>unbleached</u> fabrics.

FASHION TRENDS MAKE THINGS WORSE

To keep up with <u>rapid changes in fashion</u>, manufacturers often make <u>cheap, low quality</u> textile products that <u>don't last long</u>. These are <u>thrown away</u> when fashions change. Throwaway products <u>increase</u> textiles <u>production</u> — and <u>all</u> of the <u>problems</u> on this page.

Designers and manufacturers could design and make <u>better quality, longer lasting</u> products, that are designed to be <u>easily recyclable</u>.

ugh...stingray ties... soooo last week...

Cotton can harm the environment — I'm going commando...

Phew — a page of serious issues that are a <u>popular choice with examiners</u>. Be <u>ready</u> for them...

Textiles and the Environment

The textile industry also needs to think about how production affects the <u>people</u> involved.

You need to Consider Ethical and Moral Issues

Consumers choosing <u>not to buy</u> certain products for <u>moral</u> and <u>ethical</u> reasons is an issue for manufacturers.

ETHICAL CONCERNS

1) Textiles are often <u>produced</u> in <u>poorer</u> countries with <u>less legislation</u> about ethical working practices. Often <u>child labour</u> and <u>sweatshops</u> (where conditions and pay are terrible) are used to produce textiles <u>cheaply</u>.

2) <u>Toxic chemicals</u> — pesticides, dyes and finishes can cause <u>health problems</u> for <u>workers</u> and for some <u>consumers</u>, e.g. some kids can be sensitive to these substances.

3) Use of certain <u>animal products</u>. E.g. many people think animals shouldn't be <u>killed</u> for fur or are worried about <u>animal cruelty</u>.

SOLUTIONS — Designers and Manufacturers can...

1) Apply <u>fair trade</u> principles at all stages of the manufacturing process. This means farmers are paid a <u>fair price</u> and factory workers are given decent <u>pay</u> and <u>working conditions</u>. E.g. <u>fair trade cotton</u> is produced in this way.

2) Use fabrics made from <u>organic fibres</u> (see below). Use <u>non-toxic</u> dyes and finishes.

3) <u>Don't</u> use certain animal products — things like <u>artificial fur</u> can be used instead.

Fabrics Can be Environmentally and People Friendly

BIODEGRADABLE FIBRES

1) These fibres can be <u>broken down</u> naturally by <u>bacteria</u> and other <u>living organisms</u>, so fabrics made from them will <u>break down</u> quite <u>quickly</u> in landfill sites.

2) Plant-based fibres, like <u>cotton</u> and <u>Tencel</u>® (see p. 28), biodegrade easily.

Silk is produced by silk worms.

BIO FIBRES

1) These come from <u>biological sources</u> — plants (e.g. cotton, flax) and animals (e.g. wool, silk).

2) Biological sources are <u>renewable</u>, so bio fibres <u>don't</u> use up <u>non-renewable</u> resources.

FIBRES CAN BE GROWN ORGANICALLY

1) <u>Organic</u> fibres, (e.g. <u>organic cotton</u>) are grown <u>without</u> using <u>artificial</u> fertilisers, pesticides or herbicides.

Farming organically is better for:
- the <u>health</u> of workers — they're not exposed to toxic chemicals
- the <u>environment</u> — it doesn't harm wildlife

2) Farmers use <u>natural</u> fertilisers, such as <u>manure</u>. Instead of using herbicides, farmers weed by <u>hand</u>, and they use <u>natural</u> pesticides such as <u>spices</u>, <u>natural oils</u> and <u>soap</u>. These keep <u>pests</u> away <u>without harming</u> other creatures.

Practice Questions

1) Give <u>two</u> ways in which the textiles industry uses up the world's <u>natural resources</u>.

2) Suggest <u>two</u> ways of <u>reducing</u> the amount of <u>waste</u> from textiles products that goes into <u>landfill</u>.

3) Ian sells cushion covers made from <u>dyed cotton</u>. He's concerned that people aren't buying the covers for <u>ethical</u> reasons. Explain why people might have concerns for the health of the <u>workers</u> involved in the production of the <u>fabric</u>.

4) Tammy is designing a skirt. She chooses to make it out of <u>fair trade</u>, <u>organic</u> cotton.
   a) Explain how this fabric is <u>produced</u>.
   b) Cotton is <u>biodegradable</u>. Explain what this means.

Consumer Rights and Safety

A consumer has the right to buy a product that is of high quality and is safe. If your product's not up to scratch, people will complain, or your product could even be banned from being sold...

There are Laws to Protect Consumer Rights to Quality

In the UK, laws make sure consumers are sold quality products. These laws include...

Trade Descriptions Act — this states that any claim a manufacturer makes about their product must be true. It applies to what they say about...

- WHAT the product is made from
- HOW it has been made
- WHO made it
- What it can be USED for

The act means traders can't give false information about what they sell in writing, verbally or in an advertisement. False price reductions are also banned.

The 'one size fits all' claim proved to be false...

Sale and Supply of Goods Act 1979 — this protects consumers when they buy goods.

The goods must fit the description, be of satisfactory quality and be fit for purpose. This protects you when you buy mail order goods — i.e. the product you buy must fit the catalogue description.

Products Have to Be Safe to Use

1) The General Product Safety Regulations 2005 state that manufacturers are responsible for the safety of their products. They have to put warnings on any textile products that might be hazardous. Any goods that are thought to be dangerous can be withdrawn from sale.

2) As a designer you need to design your product to be as safe as possible for the user — by choosing suitable materials and components (see next page). You also need to make sure your manufacturing specification states the safety warnings that are needed. Some safety warnings on textiles include...

TOYS If a toy has small parts that a child could choke on (e.g. a teddy bear with button eyes) — it must be labelled:

e.g. NOT SUITABLE FOR CHILDREN UNDER 36 MONTHS
(or with wording to say that it contains small parts)

Clothing Any clothes made out of flammable fabric must be labelled:

KEEP AWAY FROM FIRE

Consumers then have a responsibility to use products for the correct purpose and follow safety warnings.

Products can be Labelled to Show They Meet Safety Standards...

Lion Mark
This shows a toy has been made by a member of the British Toy and Hobby Association who agrees to stick to strict safety, marketing and ethical guidelines.

CE Mark
This is the manufacturer's claim that the product meets the essential safety standards, allowing it to be sold throughout Europe.

Consumers might be more likely to choose your product if its label shows a safety mark.

— Text removed to protect consumer comedy rights —

It's really handy to know all the stuff on this page, so you know when you're entitled to a refund. Plus you've got the small matter of the exam to take — better read it over again, I reckon.

Consumer Rights and Safety

This rant on safety isn't quite finished yet, so I'd pop out and get another cuppa if I was you...

Furniture and Furnishings Must Meet Fire Regulations

When designing <u>furniture</u> and <u>soft furnishings</u> you need to think carefully about the type of <u>fabric</u> you use because the product has to meet <u>fire safety regulations</u>...

1) The <u>Fire Safety Regulations</u> apply to both <u>new</u> goods, and goods which are sold <u>second hand</u>.

2) They say that all <u>fabrics</u> used to cover <u>furniture</u> must be <u>resistant</u> to catching fire from matches, and if flammable natural fibres (e.g. cotton) are used then there must be a <u>non-flammable layer</u> beneath the cover fabric. Other materials used (e.g. stuffing) must not catch fire from a <u>smouldering cigarette</u>.

3) The regulations apply to <u>sofas</u> and <u>soft furnishings</u> such as cushions and pillows.

The materials are <u>tested</u> against <u>smouldering cigarettes</u> and <u>lit matches</u> — the furniture must contain <u>labels</u> to show which tests they've passed, and <u>caution</u> labels if materials are not resistant to catching fire from lit matches.

Some furnishings should be flammable...

It's Important to Choose Safe Materials

When designing a product you need to think about its <u>function</u> and <u>who's going to use it</u>. This will help you pick appropriate <u>materials</u> and <u>components</u> to make it safe.

When you're <u>designing</u> a product, ask yourself some <u>questions</u> like these...

1) **Have I selected <u>materials</u> and <u>components</u> suitable for the intended <u>function</u>?**
   E.g. is the fabric selected for protective clothing strong enough to be fit for purpose?

2) **Have I selected <u>materials</u> and <u>components</u> suitable for the intended <u>user</u>?**
   E.g. Velcro® fastenings instead of buttons (choking hazard) on clothes for small children.

3) **Are any <u>dyes</u> or <u>paints</u> safe?**   *E.g. make sure that dyes used on children's toys/clothes are non-toxic as they are likely to put the products in their mouths.*

4) **Are the <u>fabrics flammable</u>?** You need to watch out for this when combining fabrics — <u>polyester</u> has <u>low</u> flammability, however <u>cotton</u> is <u>highly flammable</u> and if cotton is <u>mixed</u> or <u>blended</u> with polyester, the resulting material will <u>still be flammable</u>.
   E.g. make nightclothes out of polyester rather than cotton.

Practice Questions

1) Name the <u>law</u> that means that any <u>claims</u> a manufacturer makes about a product have to be <u>true</u>.

2) Tom got a pair of trousers from a <u>mail order</u> catalogue, but when they arrived they were a <u>different</u> colour than that advertised in the catalogue. Which <u>law</u> protects Tom so that he can send these trousers back and get a <u>new pair</u> or a <u>refund</u>?

3) Suggest a warning that should be put on a <u>toy</u> containing <u>small parts</u> that a young child may <u>choke</u> on.

4) Jenny has designed a sofa cushion cover made from <u>cotton</u>. In order to meet the <u>Fire Safety Regulations</u>, what needs to go between this cover and the cushion?

5) Sally has made a fabric <u>baby book</u>, with pages made from polyester. She wants to make a <u>fastening</u> for the book to hold it shut. Suggest a suitable fastening and <u>explain</u> your choice.

Manufacturing Safely

Health and safety is essential for people working in textiles production — you don't want to find a finger sewn onto your new hat. So manufacturers need to carry out risk assessments and follow health and safety regulations.

Health and Safety of the Workforce is Important

1) The Health and Safety at Work Act means employers are legally responsible for the health and safety of their employees.

2) Employers must provide safety equipment and training, maintain machines, provide a safety policy and provide first aid facilities.

3) The act also makes employees responsible for using the safety equipment provided, as well as using safety guards on machines and wearing protective clothing.

Tim was given the wrong protective equipment...

Employers Must Complete a "Risk Assessment"...

1) The Health and Safety at Work Act says that businesses must complete a risk assessment for each stage of production.

2) The risk assessment will point out what must be done for the work area to be safe for employees.

3) The results of the assessment have to be checked by a Health and Safety Inspector.

> The risk assessment looks at:
> 1) Using tools and equipment.
> 2) Using materials and chemicals.
> 3) Correct protective clothing.
> 4) Safe working practices.

...To Identify and Minimise Risks

When performing a risk assessment you need to first identify any potential risks or hazards, and then put precautions in place to minimise the risk, e.g. placing warning or caution signs on machines, or erecting barriers and guards.

When you're writing a risk assessment think:

1) What could go wrong?
2) What effect would this have?
3) What can I do to prevent it happening?
3) What precautions could I take to make sure the risk is minimised?

Consider the manufacture of a leather bag:

Hazard	Precaution
1) Cutting fingers with textile cutter	Wear chainmail gloves
2) Cuts from breaking needles in thick fabric	Use guards
3) Inhalation of/skin damage from Toxic dyes	Wear goggles and rubber gloves, keep area well ventilated
4) Burning self on Iron	Make sure no-one bumps into you by using warning signs

Remember: Thread in eye of needle — not needle in eye...

Health and safety stuff is just good old common sense — but doing risk assessments is the law so it's important you know how to write them. Think: identify the risk then try to minimise it...

Manufacturing Safely

Here are the four main areas of a risk assessment — and the safety precautions that go with each. Enjoy.

1 Tools and Equipment

Sewing machines should be fitted with...

1) GUARDS to minimise the risk of stitching fingers, eye injuries caused by broken needles, etc.

2) DUST EXTRACTORS — to minimise inhalation of textile dust. They should be used with adequate ventilation.

3) Visible EMERGENCY STOP buttons in case of electrocution or accidents.

When working with scissors, craft knives and other sharp objects...

1) Take care when cutting, and use nonslip mats and steel safety rulers with craft knives.

2) Avoid injury when carrying blades by pointing the blade away from your body and attaching blade covers on knives.

3) Wear a thimble when using pins and needles and store all sharp objects safely.

2 Materials and Chemicals

1) Most chemicals will have COSHH (Control of Substances Hazardous to Health) guidelines and regulations — these will tell you:
   - what hazards the chemical presents
   - how to use, store, then dispose of the chemical safely
   - and what protective equipment to wear

2) For example, when using toxic chemicals such as dyes, finishes and solvents, you need adequate ventilation to avoid inhalation of vapours and protective clothing to protect the skin and eyes from splashes and spillages.

3) Flammable solvents (e.g. those used for cleaning and stain removal) should be kept away from sources of ignition (e.g. naked flames).

EXAM TIP
Make sure you read carefully whether the question's asking for safety measures employers or employees should take.

3 Protective Clothing

1) When using cutting machines wear chain mail gloves to protect your hands.

2) When using chemicals wear rubber gloves and goggles.

3) When sewing wear a hair net or tie long hair back to stop it from getting caught in the machine.

4) Workers using noisy machinery for a long time must wear ear protection.

4 Working Practices

1) The layout of the room should be designed with safety in mind. There must be enough space around each machine. Walkways and exits must always be kept clear, and workspaces should be kept tidy — e.g. chemicals should be put away after use.

2) There must be enough light — if possible it should be natural light.

3) Safety notices should be displayed, and safety training given to employees.

4) Employees should take regular breaks so they don't get tired and lose concentration.

5) Machinery should be well maintained and checked regularly for safety.

Practice Questions

1) Who is legally responsible for the health and safety of people in the workplace?

2) What four areas of manufacturing textiles does the risk assessment need to cover?

3) Terry is going to tie dye his T-shirt using a chemical dye that is toxic. Suggest some precautions he should take.

4) Write a risk assessment for using an industrial sewing machine.

Section Three — Environment, Society and Safety

Tools and Equipment

There are lots of hand tools to get to grips with when you're manufacturing textiles products...

Use The Right Tools For The Job

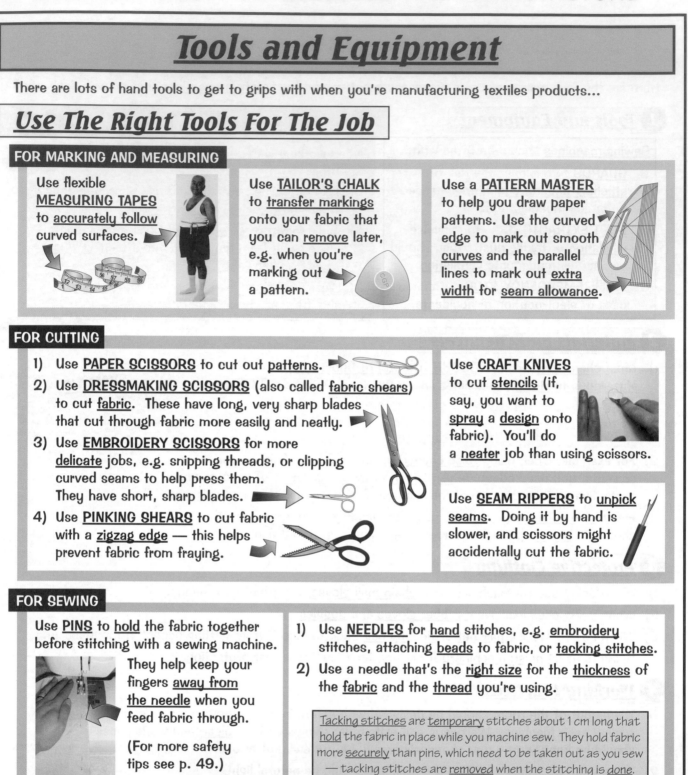

FOR MARKING AND MEASURING

Use flexible **MEASURING TAPES** to <u>accurately follow</u> curved surfaces.

Use <u>TAILOR'S CHALK</u> to <u>transfer markings</u> onto your fabric that you can <u>remove</u> later, e.g. when you're marking out a pattern.

Use a <u>PATTERN MASTER</u> to help you draw paper patterns. Use the curved edge to mark out smooth <u>curves</u> and the parallel lines to mark out <u>extra width</u> for <u>seam allowance</u>.

FOR CUTTING

1) Use <u>PAPER SCISSORS</u> to cut out <u>patterns</u>.

2) Use <u>DRESSMAKING SCISSORS</u> (also called <u>fabric shears</u>) to cut <u>fabric</u>. These have long, very sharp blades that cut through fabric more easily and neatly.

3) Use <u>EMBROIDERY SCISSORS</u> for more <u>delicate</u> jobs, e.g. snipping threads, or clipping curved seams to help press them. They have short, sharp blades.

4) Use <u>PINKING SHEARS</u> to cut fabric with a <u>zigzag edge</u> — this helps prevent fabric from fraying.

Use <u>CRAFT KNIVES</u> to cut <u>stencils</u> (if, say, you want to <u>spray</u> a <u>design</u> onto fabric). You'll do a <u>neater</u> job than using scissors.

Use <u>SEAM RIPPERS</u> to <u>unpick</u> <u>seams</u>. Doing it by hand is slower, and scissors might accidentally cut the fabric.

FOR SEWING

Use <u>PINS</u> to <u>hold</u> the fabric together before stitching with a sewing machine. They help keep your fingers <u>away from the needle</u> when you feed fabric through.

(For more safety tips see p. 49.)

1) Use <u>NEEDLES</u> for <u>hand</u> stitches, e.g. <u>embroidery</u> stitches, attaching <u>beads</u> to fabric, or <u>tacking stitches</u>.

2) Use a needle that's the <u>right size</u> for the <u>thickness</u> of the <u>fabric</u> and the <u>thread</u> you're using.

<u>Tacking stitches</u> are <u>temporary</u> stitches about 1 cm long that <u>hold</u> the fabric in place while you machine sew. They hold fabric more <u>securely</u> than pins, which need to be taken out as you sew — tacking stitches are <u>removed</u> when the stitching is <u>done</u>.

FOR PRESSING

1) <u>DRY IRONS</u> use <u>heat and pressure</u> to press creases out of the fabric and flatten seams.

2) <u>STEAM IRONS</u> are more <u>effective</u> — they use <u>water and steam</u> as well as heat and pressure.

3) Irons can also be used to <u>apply designs</u> from <u>transfers</u> onto fabric (<u>heating</u> the transfer causes the design to <u>imprint</u> onto the fabric), or to <u>fix</u> designs done with <u>fabric crayons</u> and pens.

Sewing — it seamed like a good idea at the time...

Make sure that you know exactly the <u>right tools</u> to use for these tasks. Imagine ruining your lovingly tailored creation because of a seam-unpicking disaster. Nightmare. Next it's on to the machines...

Tools and Equipment

Use Sewing Machines to Join Fabrics

Sewing machines speed up sewing, and produce neat, even stitches for a high-quality finish.

MOST SEWING MACHINES ARE LOCKSTITCH MACHINES

They use two threads — one on a bobbin under the sewing plate, the other (the top thread) on the spool pin on top of the machine. The machine interlocks the two threads to make stitches.

1) Before you start, choose the right needle for your fabric and thread thickness and fasten it securely into the machine.

2) It's a good idea to do some lines of stitching on a small sample of fabric first, so you can check:

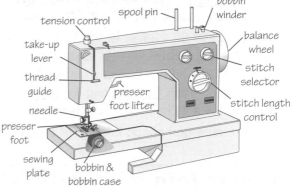

- that the thread tension is right. If the tension of the two threads is balanced then you'll get an even stitch, which isn't too tight or too loose.
- that the stitch type and stitch length are correct.

OVERLOCKERS CAN SEW SEAMS AND FINISH EDGES AT THE SAME TIME

1) Overlockers are used to finish edges to stop them from fraying. They do this by enclosing the edge, or edges, in a thread casing.

2) An overlocker works by using several top threads, but no bobbin. It also has a blade to trim the fabric edge before it's enclosed.

3) They can be used just to finish seam edges, or to sew, trim and neaten the seam all in one go.

4) They can be used for side seams in stretchy clothes like T-shirts.

Use Computerised Equipment to Add Embroidery

1) You can add decorative stitching (embroidery) using CAM (Computer-Aided Manufacture). There are a number of CAM sewing machines, e.g. the Janome Memory Craft and Pfaff Creative.

2) CAM machines can stitch designs that are already programmed into the machine.

3) You can also use CAD software (see p. 13) to produce your own designs — then save them onto a disk or memory card and transfer them to the CAM machine.

4) The fabric is secured in an embroidery hoop. The needle stays in one place while the machine moves the hoop around to create the design.

There's more on CAD/CAM on pages 54-55.

Practice Questions

1) a) What tool should you use to unpick seams, and why?   b) What about cutting thick fabric?

2) How would you attach decorative beading to a handbag?

3) When you're using a sewing machine, what three things should you check on some sample fabric before starting the real thing?

4) Why can't you use an overlocker to attach a motif to the front of a T-shirt?

5) Explain how you can use CAD/CAM to add decoration to your product.

Construction Techniques

This is what you've been waiting for — some pages about <u>making</u> stuff...

Start by Cutting Out the Pattern Pieces

1) <u>Patterns</u> are <u>templates</u> you cut round.
They're usually made of tissue paper.

2) Start by <u>laying</u> the pattern pieces out according to
the <u>lay plan</u>. The fabric might need to be <u>folded</u> so
duplicate pieces can be cut. Make sure pieces with
a <u>grain line</u> go <u>parallel</u> to the <u>selvedge</u> and pieces
with a <u>fold line</u> go exactly <u>along</u> the <u>fold</u>.

3) <u>Pin</u> at each corner and at roughly 10 cm intervals in
between. Then <u>transfer</u> any <u>markings</u> to the fabric,
using tailor's chalk or tacks (temporary stitches).

4) Make sure you <u>check</u> the layout before cutting out.

This gap is the <u>seam allowance</u>
— often 1.5 cm.

Button hole

Dart

Cutting line

Sewing line

Straight
of grain

Place
on fold

If your fabric is <u>patterned</u>, it
might need to <u>match</u> at the
seams. This might mean a
<u>less economical</u> pattern lay.

Seams Join Pieces of Fabric Together

<u>Seams</u> need to hold fabric <u>securely</u> and be <u>strong</u> enough to stand up to the <u>strains</u> put on the product.
There are different types you can use, depending on the <u>fabric</u> and <u>use</u> of the product.

Plain (Flat) Seam — the Easiest to do

1) To make a <u>flat</u> seam, take two pieces of fabric and put the <u>right</u>
sides together. Then <u>pin</u> or <u>tack</u> to hold the fabric in place.

2) Stitch about <u>1.5 cm</u> in from the edge of
the fabric (patterns have a <u>seam</u>
<u>allowance</u> to allow extra fabric for this).
<u>Strengthen</u> the seam by <u>reversing</u> back
over it for a few centimetres.

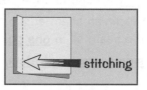

stitching

3) <u>Finish</u> the seam edges to <u>stop</u> them <u>fraying</u> (see next page).
Then <u>open</u> out the seam and <u>iron</u> so it <u>lies flat</u>.

1) <u>Plain</u> seams look <u>neat</u> on
the outside — you can only
see a thin joining line.

2) They are used for fabrics
which <u>aren't</u> going to be
under <u>too much strain</u>.

3) If your fabric is <u>stretchy</u>, use
<u>stretch or zigzag</u> stitch to
allow the seam to stretch.

French Seam — Encloses the Seam Edges

1) French seams <u>enclose</u> the <u>raw</u>
<u>edges</u> — they're used for
<u>fine</u>, <u>sheer fabrics</u>, or fabrics
which are <u>likely to fray</u>.

2) They're <u>strong</u>, but <u>not bulky</u>.
They're good for <u>baby clothes</u> — there
are no rough edges to irritate the skin.

Flat Felled Seam — Strong and Durable

1) Flat felled seams have <u>two lines</u> of <u>stitching</u>.
A plain seam is sewn and the <u>seam edges</u> are
<u>enclosed</u> by wrapping one edge around the
other, then a second line is stitched on top.

2) They <u>stop</u> edges from <u>fraying</u> and their
<u>strength</u> means they're used in hard-wearing
clothes like <u>jeans</u>. You <u>wouldn't</u> use them
with <u>delicate</u> fabrics
because of the extra <u>bulk</u>.

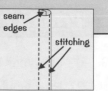

seam
edges

stitching

EXAM TIP:
If you're asked for a
<u>construction technique</u> you can
give a seam type — but make
sure you <u>justify</u> your choice.

Overlocked Seam — Quick to do

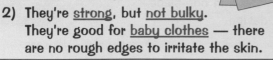

1) These are <u>strong</u> and <u>quick</u> (see next page).

2) They're good for <u>stretchy</u> clothes like T-shirts.

Imagine a world without seams — (nope, it's too terrible)...

As you'll have gathered, <u>seams</u> are pretty important in textiles and in life in general. But often you can't
just use any old one — you have to <u>think about which is best</u>. That goes for finishing edges too...

Construction Techniques

Edges can be Finished in Different Ways

The edges of fabric need to be <u>finished</u>, so the fabric <u>doesn't fray</u> or <u>lose shape</u>.

1) The <u>simplest</u> method for <u>woven</u> fabric is to cut a <u>zigzag</u> edge with <u>pinking shears</u>. ▶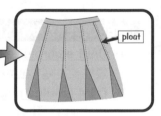
   This helps to stop the threads from <u>unravelling</u>. But for fabrics that are likely
   to fray <u>badly</u>, you'll need something a bit stronger...

2) An <u>overlocker</u> is used to <u>encase the edges</u> of fabric. See page 51 for more on
   <u>how it does this</u> and a beautiful picture of one. You can use an overlocker to
   <u>sew, trim and finish edges</u> all in one go — so it's a <u>very quick way</u> to do seams.

3) <u>Hems</u> are used to finish the <u>raw edges</u> of a product, e.g. at the bottom of a skirt or sleeves. The fabric
   is <u>folded</u> over and <u>stitched</u>. The <u>fold</u> needs to be the <u>right size</u> for the size and weight of the product.

<u>Rolled Hem</u> — fold
the edge over <u>twice</u>
so it's hidden. ➤

For <u>thicker</u> fabrics, just fold <u>once</u> so it's less
bulky. But for some fabrics you might need
to <u>finish</u> the <u>exposed</u> edge to stop it fraying.

You can Add Shape to your Products

You might want to <u>shape</u> your product so it <u>fits better</u>, or to make it look more <u>fancy</u>.

DARTS
1) These are used to <u>fit</u> a garment more <u>closely</u>
   to the body, e.g. at the waist or bust.
2) They are <u>small triangular folds</u> in the fabric

TUCKS AND PLEATS
1) Tucks and pleats are <u>folds</u> in the fabric that can either be <u>pressed</u> or <u>stitched</u>.
2) They can be used to <u>control</u> the <u>fullness</u> of fabric, e.g. make a skirt tighter
   at the waist and fuller over the hips. They can also be used to attach <u>larger</u>
   pieces of fabric to <u>smaller</u> pieces, e.g. joining sleeves.

pleat

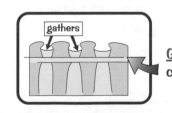

gathers

<u>GATHERS</u> — Similar to tucks and pleats, gathering is where a
couple of <u>rows</u> of stitching are <u>pulled</u> to form <u>small tucks</u>.

Practice Questions

1) How wide is a <u>seam allowance</u> usually?

2) Give <u>one advantage</u> and <u>one disadvantage</u> of using a <u>plain</u> seam to join fabric?

3) Suggest which <u>seam type</u> you would use for:
   a) a rugby shirt
   b) a silk dress
   c) cotton/Lycra® leggings

4) Why would you add <u>darts</u> to a garment?

ICT and Industrial Equipment

In industrial textiles production, most things are done by <u>big machines</u> — often <u>controlled by computers</u>.

CAD/CAM is Used a Lot in Industry

1) <u>Computer-Aided Manufacture</u> (CAM) is the process of manufacturing products with the help of <u>computers</u>. Data is downloaded from a computer to a manufacturing machine — and this data controls the machine's processes.

2) <u>CAM</u> is usually <u>linked</u> with <u>CAD</u> (Computer-Aided Design, see p. 13) — this is known as <u>CAD/CAM</u>. A product is <u>designed</u> using <u>CAD</u>, then information from the CAD software is used to <u>manufacture</u> the product using <u>CAM</u> (e.g. a CAD embroidery design is produced on a CAM embroidery machine).

3) The manufacturing machines used in CAM are <u>Computer-Numerically Controlled</u> (CNC). This means they are sent <u>data</u> in the form of numbers. The machine's on-board processor <u>interprets</u> these numbers and <u>controls</u> the <u>movements</u> of the machine.

4) These days, most <u>industrial machines</u> are <u>CAM</u> machines...

There are All Sorts of CAM Machines

CUTTING MACHINES

1) Before cutting, fabric is <u>automatically spread out</u> on the cutting table in <u>layers</u>.
2) A <u>CAM cutting machine</u> automatically cuts out the fabric pieces, following <u>CAD lay plan instructions</u>.
3) The machine cuts through <u>all the layers</u> at once, which makes the cutting process <u>really quick</u>.
4) It cuts the fabric <u>accurately</u> at <u>high speed</u> using vertical knives, high-pressure water jets or lasers.

SEWING MACHINES

1) <u>Industrial</u> sewing machines are very strong as they need to work at <u>high speeds</u>. Different machines are <u>specially designed</u> for the <u>different</u> processes involved in making a product.
2) <u>CAM</u> sewing machines are used to carry out certain processes <u>automatically</u> — e.g. sewing buttonholes and attaching pockets.

EMBROIDERY AND KNITTING MACHINES

1) <u>CAM embroidery machines</u> use <u>CAD</u> data to sew designs. They have many needles that change <u>automatically</u> as different coloured threads are needed.
2) <u>CAM knitting machines</u> use <u>CAD</u> data to control the <u>stitch pattern</u> and other design features. They can produce rolls of knitted fabric or even whole one-part garments.
3) <u>Computer control</u> makes these machines <u>very fast</u> and <u>accurate</u>, and the CAD <u>data</u> can be <u>quickly changed</u> to produce <u>new products</u>.

FABRIC PRINTERS

A <u>CAD</u> design can go directly from a computer to a <u>digital printer</u> — the design is then printed <u>directly</u> onto the fabric. This is a <u>really quick</u> method of printing onto fabric.

PLOTTER/CUTTERS — These machines use CAD data to <u>cut stencils quickly</u> and <u>accurately</u>.

PRESSING MACHINES

<u>Digital pressing machines</u> are used to improve the <u>appearance</u> of garments — they press fabric <u>flat</u> and flatten <u>seams</u> to finish the product <u>ready for sale</u>.

CAD/CAM — not a line dance where you flash your knickers...

Even though you probably won't use any machinery this big in your own work, exams have a nasty habit of asking you about <u>how CAD/CAM is used in industry</u>. Don't get caught out — learn these machines.

ICT and Industrial Equipment

CAD/CAM Has Many Advantages...

DESIGN DEVELOPMENT

1) Different designs can be quickly and cheaply modelled (see p. 13) and compared on-screen.

2) Changes to a design can be made quickly and easily.

3) Designs can be sent quickly across the world via email — so a designer can be based in a different country to the client or manufacturer.

4) Computers can be used to work out the best way to arrange pattern pieces on the fabric, so that waste is minimised. Once these layouts are saved, they're easy to reuse in the future.

MANUFACTURE

1) CAM machines speed up production processes — computer control means that processes can be done automatically, much faster than people could do them manually.

2) Machines controlled by computer are more accurate than if they were controlled by people, and processes are always done in exactly the same way. Computers can be used to monitor quality too. This means consistent, higher quality products and less wastage.

3) CAM machines don't need people to control them, just a few to oversee them, so they cut down on labour costs.

4) Workers aren't directly using dangerous machinery, so it's safer for them.

5) Computers can also be used to control stock levels, saving time, labour and storage space.

6) Computerised machines can transport materials around factories too, saving time and labour.

> All of the factors above mean that large numbers of identical, high quality products can be made quickly and efficiently — reducing manufacturing costs.

...And Some Disadvantages

1) The initial cost of software and hardware is high.
2) Workers need training in how to use CAD/CAM and this can be expensive.
3) As with all computer work, viruses, corrupt files and power cuts can destroy work.

Practice Questions

1) What does CAD/CAM mean?

2) How do CAM cutting machines cut out fabric pieces so quickly?

3) a) Describe two ways in which CAD/CAM can reduce the time needed to manufacture a product.
   b) Describe two other ways CAD/CAM can save a manufacturer money.
   c) How can using CAM machines make the workplace safer?

4) Jo is designing a knitting stitch pattern.
   She works in England, but the client she's designing for lives in Australia.
   Explain how Jo can use computers to get instant feedback on her design from her client.

5) A textiles company is in financial difficulties, with no money to spare.
   Why might getting a CAD/CAM system not be the answer to their problems?

Production Processes

There are __different ways__ of making textile products, depending on __how many__ you're going to __make__:

One-off Production is Making a Single Unique Product

1) __One-off production__ (or "__job production__") is where an __exclusive__ textile product is made to meet an __individual client's specification__ e.g. a custom-made wedding dress.

2) The product is __high-quality__ — it's made by one person or a small team, either by hand or by skilled machinists.

3) This means the product takes a __long time__ to make, and the high labour and material costs (as materials aren't bought in bulk) make it __expensive__.

Batch Production is Making a Set Number of Products

1) __Batch production__ is used to make a __specific__ number of __identical products__, called a __batch__ (e.g. 100 white fedora hats).

2) A batch can be __repeated__ as many times as is necessary.

3) Machines can be altered for each batch (e.g. to make 100 straw boaters). This means that the manufacturer can react to specific orders, and a __variety of styles__ can be made.

4) Staff have to be __flexible__ and __trained__ to deal with __different__ batches.

5) Production __costs__ are __less__ than in one-off production. Because more than one product is made, workers can repeat tasks and go quicker, and it's cheaper to buy materials in larger amounts. Also, a __batch__ could be __repeated__ in the future more easily than starting over with a new product.

6) However, batch production can be inefficient — there is time __between batches__, when equipment is being set up differently for a different style, when __nothing's being made__.

Mass Production is Making Large Numbers of Products

1) __Mass production__ (or "__volume production__") is used to make a __large quantity__ of identical products. It's used for products that'll be produced for __a long time__ with __few design changes__, e.g. socks. Products must be designed to be __suitable__ for the process (a __simple design__ in __standard sizes__).

2) Mass production is carried out using __production lines__ and __sub-assemblies__:

PRODUCTION LINES

- As a product is made, it passes through a series of __stations__. At each station a worker or machine operator does a __particular__ job (e.g. sewing buttonholes). Then they pass the product to the next station, and __repeat__ their job on an __identical product__.

- In this way __large numbers__ of products are made __quickly__.

- Workers may work on the production line in __shifts__ so that it runs __continuously__.

SUB-ASSEMBLY

- A __sub-assembly__ is a __separate__ line of manufacture that can feed into the main production line (e.g. making the strap for a bag separately before attaching it to the rest of the bag).

- Sub-assembly runs at the __same time__ as the main production line, __speeding up__ the overall process.

- It means __specialist__ machinery and specially __trained__ machinists can be used for certain stages, which means there are __fewer faults__.

3) Mass production's __expensive__ to __set up__ initially, but produces lots of identical products for a very __low cost__ per item. This is because of __economies of scale__ (see next page).

Der der der der, derder-der der der — it's batch of the day...

One-off, batch and mass production... you need to know __what they are__ and __what they're good for__.

Production Processes

Economies of Scale Reduce Manufacturing Costs

The cost of an item gets lower the more of them you produce — this is called economy of scale.
It means mass-produced products are generally cheaper than one-off products, because:

1) <u>Materials</u> and components (e.g. fastenings) can be bought in <u>bulk</u> which allows manufacturers to negotiate <u>discounts</u> — because they're buying so much.

2) Because each worker carries out a <u>specific task</u> on the production line, <u>semi-skilled</u> or <u>unskilled</u> labour can be used, <u>reducing wages</u> and <u>training costs</u>. Workers repeating the same task over and over again become <u>quick and efficient</u> at it.

3) The high cost of machines is <u>spread out</u> over the large number of products that they churn out.

4) High-volume production is often done using computer-controlled machines. Using <u>CAD/CAM</u> makes production <u>more efficient</u> (see p. 55), so it <u>reduces</u> manufacturing <u>costs</u>.

Just In Time Can Make Production More Efficient

In a <u>Just In Time</u> (JIT) system, a manufacturer gets the <u>materials</u> and <u>components</u> delivered <u>regularly</u> in <u>small amounts</u> when they're <u>needed</u>, and uses them as soon as they're delivered. There are advantages:

1) It saves on the <u>cost</u> of <u>storing</u> materials, and means there's less money <u>tied-up</u> in stock.

2) It avoids money being <u>wasted</u> through <u>stock</u> going <u>out of date</u>, or <u>unsold</u> finished products <u>piling up</u>.

BUT, <u>materials</u> and <u>components</u> must be delivered <u>on time</u> and <u>fault free</u> — there's <u>no time</u> to return poor quality materials or wait for late deliveries.

Choosing the Right Production Method is Important

When you're choosing the production method for a textiles product, think about the <u>target market</u>. Will they pay lots of money for a <u>one-off</u> item? Or will they want a <u>low-cost</u>, mass-produced item?

<u>Haute Couture</u> describes <u>one-off fashion</u> design, usually by a <u>designer fashion house</u> (e.g. John Galliano or Julien Macdonald).

Designers use the <u>highest quality fabrics</u> and <u>detailed designs</u> or <u>decoration</u> which can be very expensive. Only a <u>small number</u> of <u>very wealthy</u> people can afford these designs.

<u>"Off-the-peg"</u> clothes are bought <u>ready-to-wear</u> from a shop. These items are <u>cheaper</u> because they're mass-produced.

Designers need to think about the <u>costs of materials</u>, use more <u>straightforward designs</u> and design products in <u>standard sizes</u>.

Practice Questions

1) List two reasons why one-off production is <u>expensive</u>.

2) a) What type of production would you use to make a <u>specific quantity</u> of identical products?
   b) Explain what skills <u>workers</u> need to have for this production method.

3) What is a <u>sub-assembly</u>? Give an example.

4) Janice works in a factory that <u>mass-produces</u> trousers. Janice only knows how to fasten on the zips. Explain why it doesn't matter that Janice doesn't understand the rest of the process.

5) Describe what is meant by <u>economy of scale</u>.

6) Explain why people may be prepared to <u>pay more</u> to have their clothes manufactured using <u>one-off</u> production.

Quality Assurance and Control

If you're spending loads of money on making something, it makes sense to <u>check it's right</u>...

Quality Assurance — Setting and Meeting Standards

1) <u>Quality assurance</u> (QA) is a system that is set up to <u>make sure</u> a product meets all the criteria on the <u>design</u> and <u>product specifications</u>.

2) It's all about <u>setting standards</u> and making sure they're met — from the first design right through to the final product.

3) An important part of quality assurance is <u>quality control</u>.

4) Quality control (QC) is the process of <u>checking</u> and <u>inspecting</u> products and materials to make sure they meet all the <u>standards</u> set by the specifications.

The <u>product specification</u> is the part of the manufacturing specification that contains all the details about the product.

Quality is Checked at Critical Points

Quality control checks happen at <u>three</u> main <u>critical control points</u> during production. These checks are made on:

Raw Materials
<u>Raw materials</u> are checked to make sure that the <u>right order</u> has been <u>delivered</u> from the supplier, and that the materials are in <u>good condition</u> and meet the <u>product specification</u>.

Prototype
A final <u>prototype</u> (or sample) product will be manufactured to check that the <u>manufacturing specification</u> is exactly right. This prototype will also be compared to the <u>design specification</u> to check that all the design criteria have been met. Any problems identified when <u>making</u> the prototype will need to be <u>solved</u>, and the manufacturing specification <u>modified</u> to include the changes.

Production Samples
The <u>manufacturing specification</u> will specify <u>several points</u> in the production process where quality should be checked. At these points, a <u>sample product</u> is taken and checked (either <u>visually</u> or using a <u>computer</u>) to make sure it matches the <u>product specification</u>. If there is a fault then <u>modifications</u> need to be made (see next page).

Here's an example of a flow chart showing the stages of production for a shirt. The quality control points are shown in diamond-shaped boxes.

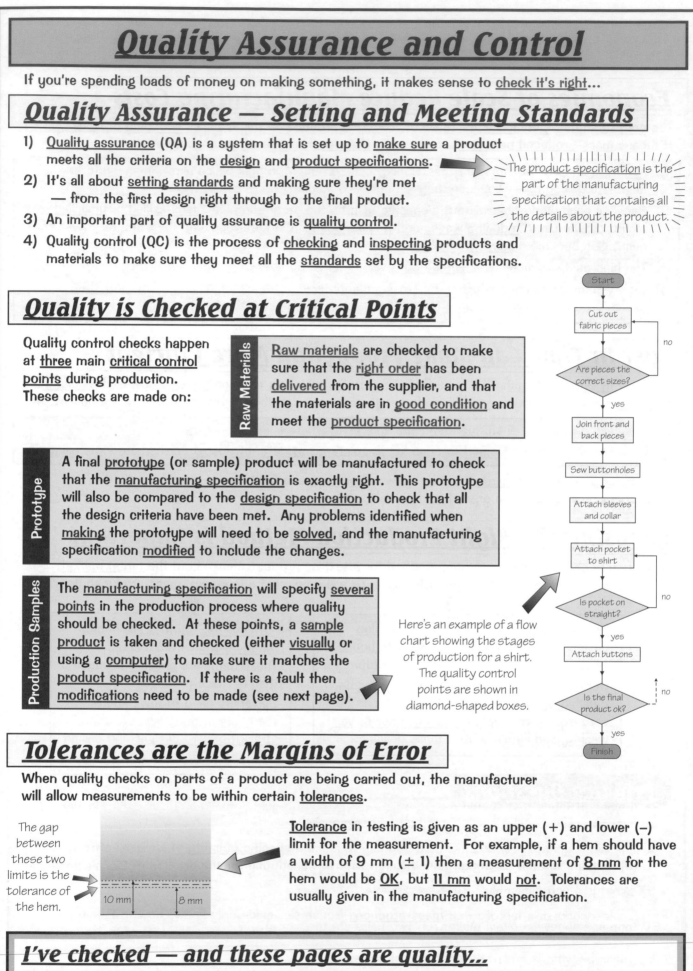

Tolerances are the Margins of Error

When quality checks on parts of a product are being carried out, the manufacturer will allow measurements to be within certain <u>tolerances</u>.

The gap between these two limits is the tolerance of the hem.

<u>Tolerance</u> in testing is given as an upper (+) and lower (−) limit for the measurement. For example, if a hem should have a width of 9 mm (± 1) then a measurement of <u>8 mm</u> for the hem would be <u>OK</u>, but <u>11 mm</u> would <u>not</u>. Tolerances are usually given in the manufacturing specification.

I've checked — and these pages are quality...

<u>Quality control</u> is all about checking that you're <u>meeting the standards</u> set in the <u>specifications</u> — a bit like what you're doing by using this book. It should mean you give quality-controlled <u>exam answers</u>.

Quality Assurance and Control

If Faults are Found, Modifications Must be Made

There's no point in a manufacturer doing all this <u>checking</u> unless any problems are <u>corrected</u>.

1) If a product's <u>not right</u>, the problem is <u>relayed back</u> to the factory floor — this is called <u>feedback</u>.

2) Feedback happens <u>straight away</u> so the problem can be fixed <u>quickly</u>.

3) Feedback usually means that a <u>modification</u> needs to be made to the <u>manufacturing process</u>.

4) These modifications are shown on a flow chart as a <u>feedback loop</u>:

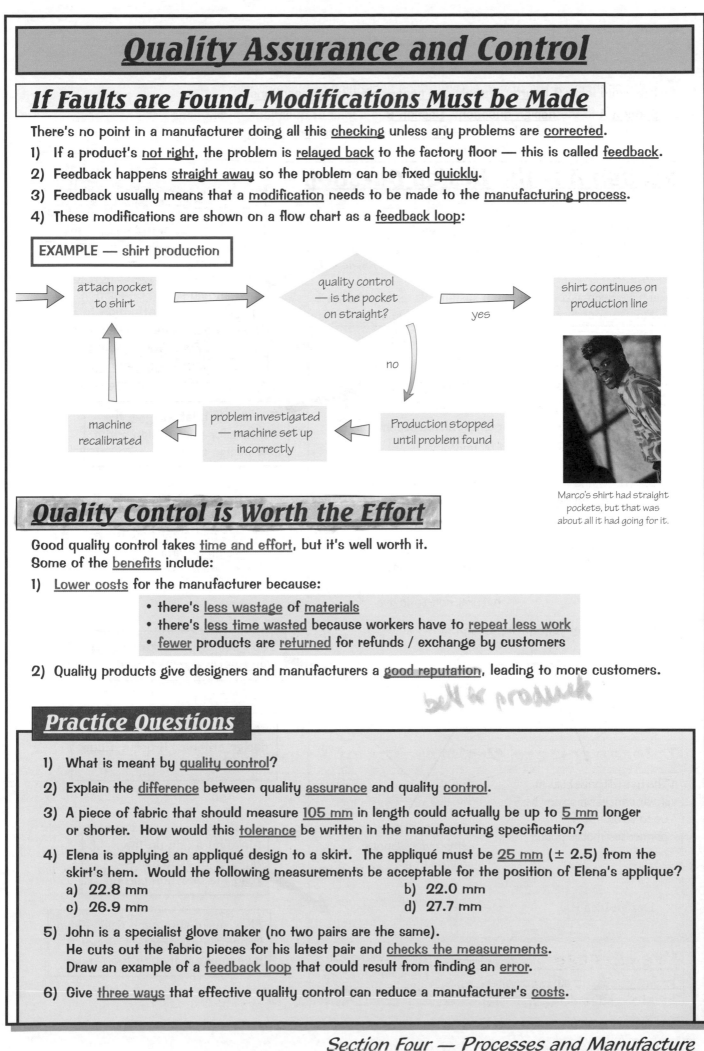

EXAMPLE — shirt production

attach pocket to shirt → quality control — is the pocket on straight? → yes → shirt continues on production line

no → Production stopped until problem found → problem investigated — machine set up incorrectly → machine recalibrated

Marco's shirt had straight pockets, but that was about all it had going for it.

Quality Control is Worth the Effort

Good quality control takes <u>time and effort</u>, but it's well worth it.
Some of the <u>benefits</u> include:

1) <u>Lower costs</u> for the manufacturer because:

- there's <u>less wastage</u> of <u>materials</u>
- there's <u>less time wasted</u> because workers have to <u>repeat less work</u>
- <u>fewer</u> products are <u>returned</u> for refunds / exchange by customers

2) Quality products give designers and manufacturers a <u>good reputation</u>, leading to more customers.

bell or product

Practice Questions

1) What is meant by <u>quality control</u>?

2) Explain the <u>difference</u> between quality <u>assurance</u> and quality <u>control</u>.

3) A piece of fabric that should measure <u>105 mm</u> in length could actually be up to <u>5 mm</u> longer or shorter. How would this <u>tolerance</u> be written in the manufacturing specification?

4) Elena is applying an appliqué design to a skirt. The appliqué must be <u>25 mm</u> (± 2.5) from the skirt's hem. Would the following measurements be acceptable for the position of Elena's applique?
   a) 22.8 mm
   b) 22.0 mm
   c) 26.9 mm
   d) 27.7 mm

5) John is a specialist glove maker (no two pairs are the same).
   He cuts out the fabric pieces for his latest pair and <u>checks the measurements</u>.
   Draw an example of a <u>feedback loop</u> that could result from finding an <u>error</u>.

6) Give <u>three ways</u> that effective quality control can reduce a manufacturer's <u>costs</u>.

Exam Technique

1) The exam lasts <u>2 hours</u>. There's <u>one paper</u> split into <u>two sections</u>.

2) <u>Section A</u> is the <u>design question</u>. Section B is a load of questions on anything and everything you've learned — <u>fibres</u>, <u>fabrics</u>, <u>processes</u>, <u>safety</u>, etc.

Section A is the Design Question

Question 1 is about designing a new product.

You are advised to spend about 30 minutes on this question.

Design Brief

You have been asked to research sustainable textiles design and to use your research to design a fashionable hat.

The hat must:

•   promote the theme of sustainability

•   be constructed using sustainable materials

•   appeal to teenagers and young adults

•   have either an appliqué or embroidered decoration

•   make use of new or smart technology

1 (a) (i)   Using a pencil, draw and label **two** different design ideas for your hat.

(2 × 3 marks)

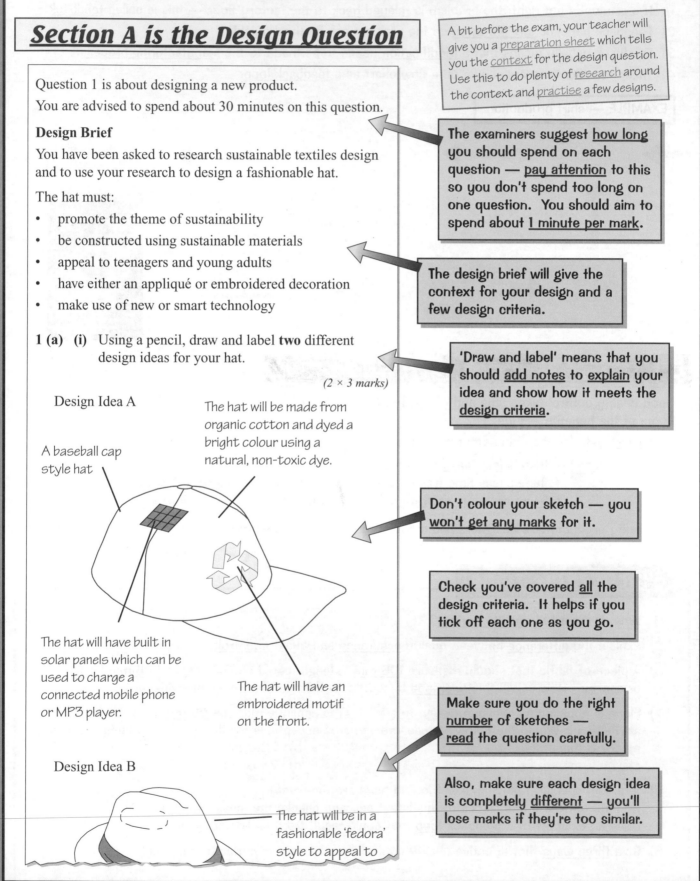

Design Idea A

A baseball cap style hat

The hat will be made from organic cotton and dyed a bright colour using a natural, non-toxic dye.

The hat will have built in solar panels which can be used to charge a connected mobile phone or MP3 player.

The hat will have an embroidered motif on the front.

Design Idea B

The hat will be in a fashionable 'fedora' style to appeal to

A bit before the exam, your teacher will give you a <u>preparation sheet</u> which tells you the <u>context</u> for the design question. Use this to do plenty of <u>research</u> around the context and <u>practise</u> a few designs.

The examiners suggest <u>how long</u> you should spend on each question — <u>pay attention</u> to this so you don't spend too long on one question. You should aim to spend about <u>1 minute per mark</u>.

The design brief will give the context for your design and a few design criteria.

'Draw and label' means that you should <u>add notes</u> to <u>explain</u> your idea and show how it meets the <u>design criteria</u>.

Don't colour your sketch — you <u>won't get any marks</u> for it.

Check you've covered <u>all</u> the design criteria. It helps if you tick off each one as you go.

Make sure you do the right <u>number</u> of sketches — <u>read</u> the question carefully.

Also, make sure each design idea is completely <u>different</u> — you'll lose marks if they're too similar.

Exam Technique

1 (a) Choose your best design idea.

Best design: ....A.............

Be careful to <u>label the sketches correctly</u> — you don't want the examiner looking at the wrong one.

(ii) Explain how the design idea you have chosen will appeal to the target market.

Portable electronic devices are very popular with teenagers, so having solar panels on the hat to charge these products will appeal to them. Many young people are concerned with issues of recycling and sustainability, so the use of organic cotton, the recycling motif and the sustainable energy to charge devices should appeal to them.

(4 marks)

You were told who the target market are in the <u>design brief</u>, so make sure that's the market you talk about.

The question's worth <u>four marks</u> so you'll need to explain your points fully.

1 (b) Use sketches, labelling and notes to present a final design for your hat. You must show a front and back view.

Marks will be awarded for:

- promotion of sustainable theme *(3 marks)*
- originality and quality of design including use of sustainable materials, use of appliqué or embroidery and use of new technology. *(8 marks)*
- use of colour *(3 marks)*
- use of fabrics and components *(4 marks)*
- presentation of final idea *(2 marks)*

The question tells you where your marks will come from, so make sure you <u>follow it carefully</u>.

Label your sketches and include <u>notes</u> to explain the fabrics, components and decorative techniques your design uses.

Embroidered recycling logo and overall green colour to promote theme of sustainability.

Interfacing used around front of hat and in peak to give the hat strength and structure.

Hat made from organic, fair trade cotton dyed green using natural, non-toxic dye. Cotton is a breathable fabric, which will make the hat more comfortable to wear.

Solar panels on both sides of the hat to charge connected devices using sustainable energy.

Make sure you include <u>both</u> a front and a back view if the question <u>asks for it</u>.

Other components include eyelets to provide ventilation (making the hat more comfortable) and an adjustable plastic press stud fastening so that hat will fit many different sized heads.

It's worth <u>20 marks</u>, so you need to include quite a lot of <u>detail</u>.

Back of hat made from a conductive fabric. This will carry electrical charge from solar panels to attached USB connector for charging devices.

When you've finished, <u>look back</u> at the design brief and check you haven't <u>missed anything</u>.

Exam Technique

Exam Technique

Here are some of the kinds of questions you'll face in Section B.

Section B Covers Everything

2 (a) Explain why many products for babies are made from a plain weave cotton fabric.

> Cotton is easily washable, which makes it
> suitable for babies' clothes and toys as they are
> likely to get dirty, and need to be washed
> frequently. It is soft and pleasant to touch and
> doesn't cause allergies, so is suitable for babies'
> sensitive skin. Plain weave fabric holds its shape
> well, so the clothes will stay in good condition
> after being washed many times.

(6 marks)

2 (b) Give two features of plain weave which make the fabric suitable for printing on.

> 1. the fabric has a smooth surface
> 2. it doesn't stretch, so doesn't create gaps

(2 marks)

2 (c) Evaluate the use of beading as a decorative technique on clothing for babies and small children.

> Beading will add interest and texture. However, the
> beads may be pulled off, so may be a choking hazard.
> They may make the products more difficult to
> wash, which is important in babies' clothes.

(3 marks)

3 Explain why you may find the following label on a textile product made from 100% cotton fabric.

> KEEP AWAY FROM FIRE
>
> To warn people that cotton is
> highly flammable.

(2 marks)

Explain means you should give a full reason why, e.g. don't just say that cotton is soft and strong — say **why** fabrics with these properties are suitable for babies.

Read the question **carefully**. There are **two parts** to answer — why the **fibre** (cotton) is suitable and why the **fabric construction** (plain weave) is suitable.

Think about all the **factors that are important** for baby products and say how the fabric **meets those requirements**.

Make sure you give **two** features. The question's only worth **two marks** in total, so you **shouldn't write loads** for each one.

Evaluate means weigh up the **good** and **bad points** about something.

Even if you think an answer is **too obvious** to be what the examiner wants, write it down anyway — some questions will be **easier** than others. There's no point looking for a complicated answer.

You'll get some marks in the exam for good **grammar**, **spelling** and **punctuation** — the front page of your exam paper tells you which question will have marks for '<u>Quality of Written Communication</u>'.

Exam Technique

4 (a) Printing is a popular method of applying colour to fabric. Briefly describe one method of hand printing.

> Flat-bed screen printing uses a screen made from a
>
> frame covered with a fine mesh, and a stencil cut from
>
> card or acetate, which is put beneath the screen. Ink is
>
> poured onto the screen and a squeegee is drawn across
>
> the screen, forcing the ink through the mesh. The
>
> screen is lifted up and the design is left on the fabric.

(3 marks)

The question says <u>briefly describe</u>, so don't give <u>too much detail</u>.

Make sure you <u>read</u> the question <u>carefully</u> — if you talk about a commercial method here instead of a hand method you'll get no marks.

4 (b) <u>Explain</u> how computers can help in the manufacture of printed fabrics.

> Designs can be created on a computer and sent
>
> directly to CAM machines to create screens and
>
> stencils for screen printing. CAD designs can also
>
> be sent to a digital printer and printed directly
>
> onto fabric. This speeds up the process of printing
>
> and improves accuracy.

(4 marks)

Underline the <u>command words</u> in a question before you answer it. Here you're being asked to <u>explain</u> something, so just writing down 'CAD/CAM' or 'it speeds it up' won't get you any marks.

5 (a) Name this piece of textiles equipment and explain what it is used for.

Name: Pinking shears

Used for: Cuts fabric with a zigzag edge to

prevent it fraying.

(2 marks)

Be <u>specific</u>. If you just put 'cutting fabric', that could describe several different tools — you need to explain what's <u>special</u> about pinking shears.

When you think you've <u>finished</u> the exam, go back and <u>read over</u> your answers to check for <u>mistakes</u>. You might even think of something else you could <u>add</u>.

Glossary

absorbent fibres / fabrics	Fibres and fabrics that are absorbent will soak up moisture.
analysis	Studying something carefully to discover and evaluate its features.
appliqué	A decoration made by cutting shapes out of fabric and attaching them on top of another piece of fabric.
batch production	The production method used to make a specific number of identical products.
biodegradable	Something that is biodegradable can be broken down by bacteria and other organisms. Biodegradable fabrics will break down quickly in landfill sites.
blended yarn	A yarn made by combining two or more types of fibre.
bonded fabric	A non-woven fabric made from fibres held together, e.g. by glue, stitching or heat.
CAD/CAM	Computer-Aided Design linked directly to Computer-Aided Manufacture.
calendering	A finish applied to fabrics using heavy heated rollers which squash the fabric, making it smooth and shiny.
client	Someone who's paying for a service such as a clothing design.
components	Pre-manufactured parts that are added to fabrics to make textile products, e.g. zips, buttons, laces.
construction	The way something's been put together (or the process of putting something together).
consumer	A person who buys something to use themselves.
delicate	Describes an object or material that is easily broken or damaged.
design specification	A list of characteristics that a product should have.
disassembly	Taking something to pieces to see how it was put together.
drape	How a fabric falls or hangs.
dry cleaning	A method of cleaning fabrics using solvents (a type of chemical) instead of water.
dye	A substance used to add colour to large areas of a fabric.
efficient production	Producing something with the minimum amount of time, energy or materials.
elasticity	Things have elasticity if they can be stretched and return to their original shape.

Glossary

embroidery	Decorative stitching applied to a fabric by hand or machine.
ethical and moral issues	Issues which many people have views about whether they're right or wrong.
evaluation	Looking at what you've done to see if you have accomplished everything you set out to do, and deciding what went well and what went badly.
fabric	A sheet of material made from yarns or fibres held together by weaving, knitting, bonding or felting.
felt	A non-woven fabric made by combining pressure, moisture and heat to interlock a mat of wool fibres.
fibre	A thin, hair-like strand. Fibres can either be spun into yarns, or used as they are, to make fabrics.
finish	A treatment applied to fabric at the end of manufacture to give it beneficial qualities.
finite resource	One that will eventually run out.
fit for purpose	Something that is fit for purpose must do the job it has been designed to do.
flammability	How easily something catches fire.
garment	A piece of clothing.
gutta	A resist used in silk painting.
haberdasher	Someone who sells buttons, zips and other small things for sewing.
industrial production	Large scale production by companies.
interfacing	A layer of fabric hidden inside a textile product to give strength, stability or support to an area, e.g. in collars or around buttonholes.
knitted fabric	A fabric made from yarns held together by interlocking loops.
lamination	Sticking together two or more layers of fabric in order to produce a fabric with better properties. E.g. a GORE-TEX® product is made by laminating a GORE-TEX® membrane between an outer and an inner layer of fabric to make the product sturdier.
landfill	Rubbish buried in the ground.
lay plan	A plan that shows you how to position pattern pieces on fabric in the most efficient way.

Glossary

lining	A layer of fabric on the <u>inside</u> of something.
loom	A machine for <u>weaving</u> yarns into fabric.
manual process	Doing something <u>by hand</u>.
manufacturing specification	This tells a manufacturer <u>exactly how</u> to make a product.
marketable	A marketable product is one that's <u>in demand</u> — it should <u>sell well</u>.
mass production	The <u>production method</u> used to produce a <u>large number of identical products</u> using a production line.
mechanical process	Using a <u>machine</u> to do something.
micro-encapsulation	The process of <u>embedding</u> small amounts of chemicals in a fabric to give the fabric <u>beneficial qualities</u>.
microfibres	Really <u>thin</u> synthetic fibres, up to 100 times thinner than a human hair.
mixed fabric	A fabric that has been made using <u>more than one</u> type of <u>yarn</u>.
motifs	<u>Small fabric badges</u> that are sewn onto fabric to <u>add decoration</u>.
nanomaterial	In textiles, nanomaterials are fabrics that have been made from <u>nanofibres</u> (very very very thin fibres) or fabrics that have been <u>treated</u> using <u>nanotechnology</u>.
one-off production	Making a <u>single</u>, <u>unique</u> product.
organic fibres	Fibres from crops grown <u>without</u> using <u>man-made pesticides, herbicides</u> and <u>fertilisers</u>.
overlocker	A type of sewing machine that <u>trims the fabric edge</u> and <u>encases it in thread</u>.
photochromic dyes	Dyes that <u>change colour</u> in response to changes in <u>light conditions</u>.
polymer	A long <u>chain</u> of small molecules joined end-to-end. They can be used to make synthetic fibres.
prototype	A <u>full scale model</u> of a design used to test things like size, shape and manufacturing methods.
quality assurance	The <u>system</u> that is set up to make sure that <u>high quality</u> products are produced.
quality control	The <u>checks</u> that are carried out on materials and products before, during and after production to make sure that standards are being met.

Glossary

regenerated fibres	Made from <u>natural materials</u>, which are treated with <u>chemicals</u> to produce fibres. E.g. viscose is made from chemically treated cellulose.
resist	Something which <u>prevents</u> dye from reaching parts of a fabric.
resources	Things that you need to <u>make stuff</u>, e.g. oil is a resource that's needed for making polyester and for producing energy.
risk assessment	<u>Identifying</u> the <u>potential hazards</u> at each stage of production and the <u>precautions</u> which need to be taken to minimise risks.
smart fabric	A fabric which <u>changes its properties</u> in response to its surroundings.
squeegee	A tool used in screen printing to <u>spread</u> printing ink and <u>force</u> it <u>through</u> the screen.
staple fibre	A <u>short</u> fibre, e.g. cotton fibres are staple fibres.
sub-assembly	A <u>separate line of manufacture</u> which runs at the same time as the main production line, and eventually feeds into it.
sustainable	A sustainable process or material is one that can be used <u>without causing permanent damage</u> to the environment or <u>using up finite resources</u>. E.g. sustainable wood comes from forests where fast-growing trees are chopped down and replaced.
synthetic	Something that is <u>entirely man-made</u>.
thermochromic dyes	Dyes that <u>change colour</u> in response to <u>changes in temperature</u>.
tolerance	The <u>margin of error</u> allowed for a measurement of part of a product. Tolerances are usually given as an upper and lower limit, e.g. 23 mm ($\pm$ 2).
toxic	Describes something that is <u>harmful</u> to living creatures.
trimmings	In textiles, <u>components</u> such as <u>laces</u>, <u>ribbons</u>, <u>braid</u>, <u>lace</u>, <u>beads</u> and <u>sequins</u>. In cuisine, the accompaniments to the meat in a roast dinner, such as vegetables, roast potatoes, Yorkshire puddings and stuffing.
upholstery	Textile products used to <u>cover</u> and <u>cushion furniture</u>, such as sofa covers and stuffings.
versatile	Something that is <u>suitable</u> for lots of <u>different</u> uses.
woven fabric	A fabric made by <u>interlacing two sets of yarns</u> together.
yarn	A <u>thread</u> made by <u>twisting fibres together</u>.

Answers

Page 5 — Product Analysis and Trends

1) A client, to briefly tell a designer what kind of product they want.

2) a) It will give her ideas about — two from, e.g: suitable designs / materials / manufacturing techniques / how to make her product suitable for the target market.
   b) Three from e.g. components / materials / shape / decoration / price / construction / fitness for purpose.
   c) By taking the hats apart she can find out how the parts were put together and what order they were put together in. It will also show her how any decoration was added to the hats.

3) a) To find out which styles are selling well and which aren't, and the most popular price for shirts. He can use this information in his own design.
   b) By looking at trend forecasts for styles, fabrics and colours, to make sure the ones he chooses will be up-to-date.

Page 7 — Market Research

1) a) Target group (or market)
   b) Three from, e.g: do they like a particular style / how much are they willing to pay / where do they buy them from / is there something they'd like that doesn't already exist?

2) a) Yes, Peter is right. Jordan is using closed questions, with no follow-up, so a questionnaire will quickly get her clear results that are easy to analyse.
   b) She'll get more ideas and more detailed information about the sort of beach shoes people want. However, collecting the information might be quite time-consuming and she could end up with information about lots of different types of shoes, which could be hard to analyse.

Page 9 — Consumer Choice and Product Design

1) E.g. fashions can change several times a season, so people buy clothes more often / people might want to follow short-lived celebrity trends / modern manufacturing systems can make clothes quickly and cheaply, so clothes can be bought more cheaply.

2) Less ethical manufacturers may employ child labour, pay their workers less, and spend less on ensuring their workers' safety. This reduces their costs, meaning they can sell their products more cheaply.

3) E.g. use fabric made from renewable fibres, such as biofibres, minimise waste and pollution when making products.

Page 11 — Generating Design Ideas

1) Analyse and summarise the data.

2) Five from, e.g: the fabric should be absorbent / quick drying / easily washable / hard wearing / it should measure 40-50 x 60-70 cm / it should show the CGP logo / RRP should be 50p or less / it should have funny pictures and bad jokes on it.

3) a) Working from existing products is a good start here, because you need to make something with the same basic structure, but with a few modifications.
   b) A mood board would be useful here, because the basic forms of the covers are established, but the decoration and style can be inspired by a range of Art Deco images.

Page 13 — Generating Design Ideas

1) The sketches are drawn and coloured roughly, so they're not very clear. The labels aren't sufficient to explain fully the features of the product. The two ideas are very similar. The products look like they would be impractical to make.

2) Two from: produce mood boards / draw and annotate your designs / design fabric decoration, e.g. logos / model designs in 3D to see what they'll look like.

3) Designs can be produced using CAD, then presented to the client using a virtual catwalk. Designs can be emailed to the client as they're modified, so the client is aware of how the product is changing.

Page 15 — Development

1) the design specification

2) By asking people who might be likely to buy them.

3) A prototype is a full-scale model of a product design.

4) Three from, e.g: to test the sizes and shapes of designs / to check on methods of manufacture / to check for potential manufacturing problems / to work out the costs of mass production / to work out manufacturing time required for mass production / to plan the equipment and labour required for mass production / to get feedback from the client or target group.

Answers

5) a) To see if it's fit for purpose, if it's appealing to the target market and if they would consider buying it.
   b) The client, to check it's what they wanted. Experts in the textiles industry, to see if they have any suggestions for improvements.

Page 17 — Development

1) So you don't produce a design that doesn't fit the design specification because it's too expensive to make.

2) Three from, e.g: materials / components / labour / energy / waste disposal / equipment / packaging / transporting products.

3) E.g. the workforce might need to be paid more for working overtime in order to meet the deadlines. More money might need to be spent on equipment required to speed up the manufacturing process.

4) E.g. Paulo could reduce the number of pleats, so the skirt is quicker and easier to make. He could also simplify the decoration — e.g. by removing the beading or simplifying the embroidery, so the design can easily be stitched by machine.

5) a) Throughout the design process, the design is modelled, tested, evaluated and modified, to make sure it meets the design specification.
   b) Quality products should mean more sales, which will benefit the client. Quality products will also enhance the reputations of both the designer and the client.

6) the design specification

Page 19 — Planning for Production

1) manufacturing instructions

2) E.g. types of fabric, precise amounts needed, colours, any special features such as finishes.

3) The tolerance is the margin of error for a measurement.

4) a) Where a quality control check should take place.
   b) The equipment needed to do the cutting and how long it should take.

Page 21 — Types of Fibre

1) filaments

2) Staple fibres. The yarn looks hairy, rather than smooth, which suggests it's made from lots of short fibres.

3) They come from renewable sources and the fibres are biodegradable and often recyclable.

4) Wool fibres are harvested from the fleece of a sheep or other animal. The fibres are cleaned and straightened, and then spun into a yarn.

5) Chemically treated cellulose

6) E.g. they're resistant to biological damage and can be set into shapes, like pleats. (There are lots of other possible answers.)

7) Synthetic fibres are difficult to dye because they aren't very absorbent.

8) bran flakes (just)

Page 23 — Fabric Construction

1) a) right to left
   b) up and down

2) It's where the weft yarns wrap around the warp yarns, at the edge of the fabric.

3) a) plain
   b) twill
   c) satin

4) warp-knitted fabric

Page 25 — Fibres and Fabrics

1) a) cotton
   b) E.g. wool (cotton or some synthetic fibres can also be used).
   c) E.g. silk (cotton or polyester can also be used).

2) a) Positive: two from, e.g: strong / hard-wearing / absorbent / comfortable / cool in hot weather / easy to wash / easy to add colour to / doesn't cause allergies / non-static
   Negative: two from, e.g. creases easily / highly flammable / poor elasticity / can shrink when washed / dries slowly.
   b) Positive: two from, e.g: warm / absorbent / good elasticity / low flammability / crease resistant.
   Negative: two from, e.g. can shrink when washed / dries slowly / can feel itchy.

3) a) elastane (LYCRA®)
   b) Positive: e.g. extremely elastic / strong / hard-wearing / lightweight / keeps shape / resists sun damage / resists biological damage.
   Negative: e.g. not absorbent / highly flammable / not biodegradable.

4) E.g. it has low flammability, which is an important safety feature in night clothes / it has good elasticity, which helps make clothes comfortable.

5) a) cotton or linen
   b) E.g. it creases easily, or it has poor elasticity.

Answers

6) E.g. can feel itchy / can shrink when washed / dries slowly.
E.g. polyester / cotton / silk / viscose would be better.

Page 27 — Combining Fibres in Fabrics

1) Any four from, e.g: change appearance / create interesting colour or texture effects / improve practical qualities / improve working qualities / make fabric cheaper to produce.

2) synthetic fibres

3) Blending — different fibres are spun together to make a yarn. Mixing — different yarns are used together to make a fabric.

4) Three from, e.g: the fabric is stronger / less absorbent, so dries more quickly / is less likely to crease / is less likely to shrink.

5) Thick nylon fibres are woven into cotton, silk or polyester.

Page 29 — New Fabrics and Technologies

1) a) Nomex®
   b) Kevlar®

2) E.g. in clothes with built-in sensors to monitor things like heart rate, to make washable electronic switches to go in clothing, in heated clothing, e.g. motorbike clothing.

3) A smart fabric reacts automatically to changes in the surroundings.

4) Microcapsules of insect repellent could be embedded in the fabric.

Page 31 — Choosing Fabrics

1) Does the job it's designed to do.

2) a) e.g. warmth, wool or acrylic, knitted
   b) e.g. durability, polyester, plain-woven
   c) e.g. appearance, silk, satin-woven
   d) e.g. comfort, cotton, satin-woven
   e) e.g. stain resistance or durability, nylon, woven

3) A list of criteria that the fabric for a particular product must meet.

4) a) e.g. two from: good insulator / easy to wash / low flammability
   b) e.g. strong, durable
   c) e.g. soft, easy to wash
   d) e.g. comfortable, smooth

Page 33 — Fabric Maintenance

1) fibre content

2) a) e.g. wool
   b) e.g. linen

3) They should be reshaped and laid out flat while damp. This is so they don't stretch.

4) Some fabrics will melt, burn or shrink, if the iron is too hot. Others will remain creased if the iron is too cold.

5) E.g. fabrics that lose their shape when they absorb water should be dry-cleaned. Some tailored garments should be dry-cleaned so the interfacings don't shrink. If oil or grease needs to be removed, dry cleaning will be more effective than conventional washing.

Page 35 — Dyeing

1) They're cheaper and the colours are brighter and more consistent.

2) a) To even out the colour before dyeing, so that the dyed fabric will be an even colour.
   b) To fix the dye so it won't come out in the wash.

3) a) batik
   b) James could use a fabric made from natural fibres. This would be more absorbent, so would take up the wax and dye better.

Page 37 — Printing

1) Because they have a smooth surface and no surface pattern to detract from the design.

2) a) block printing
   b) E.g. he can use the same block to repeat the design many times, but it takes a long time to make the block.

3) a) A screen is made for each colour needed in the design. The fabric moves on a conveyor belt under the screens. Ink is applied to each screen and forced through to the fabric by metal rods that move across the screens. The screens are lifted and the fabric moves on to its next position.
   b) It can take a long time to make the screens and it's expensive to buy and set up the machinery.

Answers

Page 39 — Decoration and Enhancement

1) a) appliqué
   b) Two from, e.g: use non-woven fabrics / use a fusible interface like bondaweb / fold the edges under before stitching.
2) a) stitching
   b) top fabric
   c) wadding
   d) bottom fabric
   e) warmth
3) a) decoration
   b) E.g. the stitching can be easily damaged.

Page 41 — Fabric Finishes

1) To change the appearance, texture, wearing properties or after care characteristics of the product.
2) The finish could be washed out if the overalls aren't washed correctly.
3) By removing the scales from wool fibres that tangle and lock together when the garment is washed, causing it to shrink.
4) a) Mechanical finishes are finishes that are created with the use of machines.
   b) Mechanical finishes are cheaper to do than chemical finishes.

Page 43 — Manufactured Components

1) Trouser zips are fixed at one end, but coat zips are not.
2) The hooks can collect fibres, which makes them stick less well to the loops.
3) a) buttons
   b) E.g. they can fall off and can be damaged when washed.
4) a) They are extra layers of fabric hidden inside a product to give it strength, stability and support.
   b) It can be stuck to fabric by being heated.

Page 45 — Textiles and the Environment

1) Two from, e.g: coal and oil are burned to provide energy used in production / oil is used to make polyester / large amounts of water are used in manufacturing processes.
2) Two from: recycle waste fabric / reduce packaging / reuse products.
3) They might be suffering health problems from contact with pesticides from cotton production or toxic dyes.

4) a) Organic cotton is farmed without using artificial fertilisers, pesticides or herbicides. Natural fertilisers like manure and natural pesticides are used instead. Weeding is done by hand. Fair trade means farmers are paid a fair price and factory workers get decent pay and working conditions.
   b) The fibres are broken down naturally by bacteria and other living organisms.

Page 47 — Consumer Rights and Safety

1) Trade Descriptions Act
2) Sale and Supply of Goods Act
3) E.g. 'Not suitable for children under 36 months'.
4) A layer of non flammable fabric.
5) E.g. Velcro® because it's soft and it isn't a choking hazard.

Page 49 — Manufacturing Safely

1) The employer
2) Using tools and equipment, using materials and chemicals, correct protective clothing, safe working practices.
3) Wear rubber gloves and goggles, ensure adequate ventilation.
4) Hazards, e.g:
   Stitching fingers / eye injuries — use machine guards.
   Inhalation of textile dust — use dust extractors and have adequate ventilation.
   Getting long hair trapped in machine — use hair nets or tie hair back.
   Injuries from being knocked — ensure adequate space around work area.
   Hearing damage from noisy machines — wear ear protection.

Page 51 — Tools and Equipment

1) a) Seam rippers — they're faster than doing it by hand, and won't cut the fabric like scissors could.
   b) Dressmaking scissors (fabric shears) because they have long, sharp blades.
2) By hand-stitching, with a needle and thread.
3) The thread tension, the stitch type, the stitch length.
4) Overlockers trim the fabric as they go, so they can't be used for attaching motifs to fabric.
5) You could add embroidery. Computers have software so that you can produce your own designs, which can be transferred to the machine, and reproduced accurately.

Answers

Page 53 — Construction Techniques

1) 1.5 cm

2) E.g. they're easy to do / look neat on the outside / can be made to lie flat. But they aren't good at bearing strain / aren't very stretchy.

3) a) flat felled seam
   b) french seam
   c) overlocked seam

4) To fit it more closely to the body.

Page 55 — ICT and Industrial Equipment

1) Computer-Aided Design linked directly to Computer-Aided Manufacture.

2) They cut through many layers at once and automatically follow a computerised plan.

3) a) Two from, e.g: CAM machines work faster than manually-controlled machines / computerised machines can transport goods around the factory to where they're needed / CAM machines are more accurate, so less time is spent repeating work.
   b) E.g. fewer people are needed to control the machines, saving on labour costs. CAD software minimises the amount of waste fabric by finding the best way to lay out patterns.
   c) People don't need to directly handle the machinery — they work at a "safe distance".

4) It could be designed using CAD software, and the design emailed to the client so they could check it was what they wanted. Then they could email their feedback.

5) It costs a lot to buy and set up the machines, and to train workers to use them.

Page 57 — Production Processes

1) E.g. high labour costs (because things take highly-skilled people a long time to make) and greater material costs (because materials are high quality and bought in smaller quantities).

2) a) batch production
   b) They need to be flexible so they can switch from making one thing to making another as quickly as possible.

3) A separate production line making a part of a product which is then attached to the main product. Examples could include bag straps, trouser pockets, shirt collars — anything where part of a product has to be assembled before it can be attached to the main product.

4) In mass production, each worker on a production line only performs one job before passing the product on.

5) Economy of scale is where the cost of an item gets lower the more of them you produce.

6) People who can afford it are prepared to pay more for a unique garment that has been designed to their requirements and which fits them perfectly.

Page 59 — Quality Assurance and Control

1) Quality control is the process of checking and inspecting products and materials to make sure they meet all the standards set by the specifications.

2) Quality assurance is all about setting standards for quality and making sure they're met. Quality control is how you check that you're meeting those standards.

3) 105 mm (± 5)

4) a) yes
   b) no
   c) yes
   d) no

5) E.g.

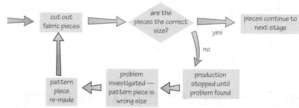

6) There will be less wastage of raw materials, less time wasted by workers repeating work, and fewer products returned by customers for refunds or exchanges.

Index

Index

F

fabric brushing 41
fabric
  care labels 32
  construction 22-23
  finishes 40-41
  fitness for purpose 30
  maintenance 32-33
  printers 54
  properties 24-25
  specification 31
  types 24-25
fair trade 45
fashion trends 5, 8, 44
fastenings 42
FASTSKIN® swimsuits 28
feedback (in manufacturing processes) 59
felt 22, 24
felted fabrics 22
fibres
  properties 24-25
  types 20–21
filaments 20
fire safety regulations 47
fit for purpose 30
flammability 24-25, 27, 30, 40
flame retardant finishes 40
flat felled seams 52
flat-bed screen printing 36
flow charts 19
french seams 52

G

gabardine 24
gathers 53
GORE-TEX® 8, 28
gutta 35

H

hand dyeing 35
Harris tweed 24
haute couture 57
Health and Safety at Work Act 48
hems 53

I

ICT (information communication technology)
  7, 13, 54-55
industrial equipment 54–55
interfacings 43
International Textile Care
  Labelling Code (ITCLC) 32
interviews 7
ironing 33
irons 50

J

James Bond 21
jersey 24
Jim the porpoise 30
JIT (just-in-time) production 57
job production 56

K

kangaroo pouch 11
Kevlar® 28
knitted fabrics 23-24
knitting machines 54

L

labels 32-33, 43, 46
laminated fabrics 28
lay plan 13, 18, 52
linen 20, 24
lion mark 46
lockstitch machines 51
LYCRA® 21, 25, 27

M

manufactured components 42-43
manufacturing
  costs 16
  instructions 18
  processes 31, 56-57
  specification 18, 58-59
market research 6-7
marketability 4
mass production 56
measuring tapes 50
mechanical finishes 41
micro-encapsulation 28

Index

Index